STAFFORDSHIRE LIBRARY AND INFORMATION SERVICES
Please return or renew by the last date shown

If not required by other readers, this item may may be renewed
in person, by post or telephone, online or by email.
To renew, either the book or ticket are required

24 HOUR RENEWAL LINE 0845 33 00 740

World Faiths

BUDDHISM

Mel Thompson

Chrysalis Children's Books

WORLD FAITHS

BUDDHISM   CHRISTIANITY
HINDUISM   ISLAM
JUDAISM   SIKHISM

First published in the UK in 2003 by
Chrysalis Children's Books
An imprint of Chrysalis Books Group Plc
The Chrysalis Building, Bramley Road,
London W10 6SP

Paperback edition first published in 2005

Produced by Bender Richardson White, PO Box 266, Uxbridge, UB9 5NX

Editorial Manager: Joyce Bentley   Senior Editor: Sarah Nunn
Project Editor: Lionel Bender   Text Editors: Michael March, Peter Harrison
Designer: Richard Johnson   Art Editor: Ben White
Proofreader: Jennifer Smart   Production: Kim Richardson
Picture Researchers: Joanne O'Brien at Circa Photo Library, and Cathy Stastny
Cover Make-up: Mike Pilley, Radius   Indexer: Peter Harrison
Diagrams and maps: Stefan Chabluk

Thanks to Joanne O'Brien at ICOREC, Manchester, for planning the structure and content
of these books.

ISBN: 1 84138 710 X (hb)
ISBN: 1 84458 461 5 (pb)

British Library Cataloguing in Publication Data for this book is available from
the British Library.

Printed in China

10 9 8 7 6 5 4 3 2 1

Picture Acknowledgements
We wish to thank the following individuals and organizations for their help and assistance, and for
supplying material in their collections: Circa Photo Library: pages 5 bottom, 12, 14, 23, 47, 48–49,
52–53 ; (Rebecca Thompson) 1, 3, 5 top, 19, 22, 25, 26, 28, 36, 38, 54–55; (William Holtby) cover,
5 bottom, 7, 9, 11, 13, 15, 18, 20, 21, 29, 30, 32, 33, 35, 37, 39, 40, 46, 50–51; (John Smith) 44;
(T. Halbertsma) 41. Corbis Images: (Tim Page) 27. Lionheart Books: (NASA) 6–7; (BRW) 34. Rebecca
Thompson: 4. Topham Photo Library: (Image Works) 8, 16, 17, 42; (Picturepoint)10, 31; (Photri) 43;
(Press Association) 45.

CONTENTS

A Buddhist Family

Nigel lives with his wife and daughter near Oxford in England. He was born and brought up in the Christian faith, but converted to Buddhism while he was engaged to Duan, a Buddhist from Thailand.

'DUAN AND I have come to visit the Buddhist temple in Wimbledon, south London, with our daughter, Samantha. The temple is built in the style of Buddhist temples found in Thailand.

In the warm sunshine of Thailand, the Eastern architecture of the temple and the orange robes of the monks seem normal, but set against grey English skies here in Oxford, they look unfamiliar. Many who worship at the temple have connections with Thailand; others are Westerners who have chosen to practise Buddhism. Not all these people visit the temple regularly, but they attend the major festivals, to listen to talks given by the monks and make offerings.

Duan and I have been regular attenders since before Samantha was born. We try to visit the temple once a week. Samantha attends a class for schoolchildren, where she learns not only about Buddhism but how to play a Thai musical instrument.

When she was younger, Samantha went to a nursery room in the temple, where she and other girls and boys would act in plays about the Buddha, the founder of Buddhism. They also drew and painted pictures.

At home we have a small shrine, with statues of the Buddha. Sometimes our family members put flowers on the shrine, leaving them there until they wither, as a reminder that even the most beautiful of things will fade and die. As Buddhists, we try to follow the basic Buddhist teachings on how to live, but, like most Thai Buddhists, we are not vegetarians. In many respects, our family is no different from any other.

At school, Samantha attends religious education lessons and joins in morning assembly. Although she thinks of herself as a Buddhist, she does not mind joining in with other people's religions. To a Buddhist it does not matter how religious you are; what counts is how you live your life. You should not kill, steal, eat too much, tell lies, or get drunk.

Buddhists think that their teachings are mostly common sense.'

Buddhists worldwide

The number of Buddhists worldwide is estimated at 360 million, most of whom live in South-east Asia.

ASIA
Most Buddhists live in South Asia, South-east Asia and the Far East. In the East, different countries have different Buddhist traditions. For example, Buddhism in Thailand differs from the Buddhism found in Japan or Tibet.

THE WEST
There are Buddhists all over the world. Some of those in Europe and the USA have come from traditionally Buddhist countries; others are westerners who have chosen to follow the Buddhist path.

KINDS OF BUDDHISM
In the west, people can choose from the different kinds of Buddhism, such as Zen, Theravada or Tibetan Buddhism. They can also join Buddhist groups that try to make Buddhism particularly relevant for Westerners.

What Do Buddhists Believe?

There is no fixed self, Buddhists say. Life depends on other people, and on circumstances over which we have no control. If you were born of the opposite sex, in a different country, to different parents, or if you were very rich or very poor, your life would be different. None of us has a fixed or permanent self, and as our circumstances change, so will we.

THE BUDDHA'S TEACHING is known as *Dharma*. It is the Dharma that helps people see life as it really is. It teaches the Three Universal Truths about life:

1. There is only one thing you can say for certain: everything changes. People are born, they grow old, they die. Places change; rocks wear away, even stars grow old. Nothing lasts forever.

2. Nothing and nobody has a fixed or permanent 'self', because everything, including our sense of who we are, depends on everything else. There is no real 'you' that is separate from the things that you do, say, or think. Everyone is part of a world in which everything and everyone else is interconnected.

3. Anything may cause you disappointment. Everything changes, you cannot be in total control of your life, and things will not always work out the way you would wish. We all have our limitations. Eventually everyone has to face illness, old age and death. Even pleasures can disappoint, because they do not last. Human life therefore is inescapably bound up with suffering and disappointment – which Buddhists call *Dukkha*.

Science tells us that everything in the universe is in a state of change: even galaxies are born and die. Belief that everything changes was also the starting point for the Buddha's teaching.

Just as the lotus grows through mud and water to open out into the sunlight, so, Buddhists believe, the human mind can open out and flower. The lotus is a symbol for the awakening mind.

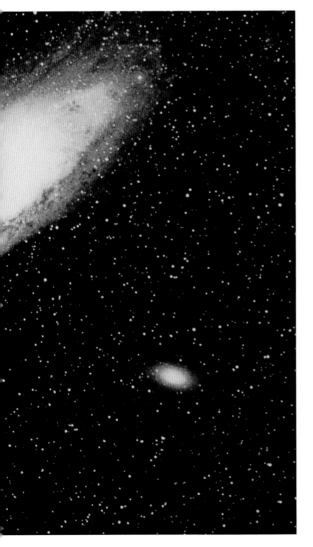

Can we avoid disappointment?

Like a doctor prescribing a cure for an illness, the Buddha set out a way to overcome Dukkha. It is known as the Four Noble Truths:

1 Everything in life may involve disappointment and suffering.
2 Disappointment occurs because we long for things to be different; we crave things we cannot have.
3 If we stop craving the impossible, learn from things that go wrong and enjoy our life in spite of its limitations, we can achieve happiness.
4 The way to stop craving is to follow the Noble Eightfold Path. This is a series of steps expressing wisdom, practical action and mental skill.

Open to all

Those who follow the Dharma do not believe it sets them apart from others. They tend not to use labels such as 'Christian' or 'Buddhist' or 'religious', but see Dharma as something that anyone can explore and act on to their own advantage.

Students in a discussion group with their teacher. Buddhists believe that everyone's thoughts and actions are inter-related. We shape our own lives by our karma.

Does everything have a cause?

Everything is the result of an infinite number of causes, Buddhists say. Everything is interconnected, so anything that comes into being does so from causes and conditions. When one thing changes, everything else changes, and when one thing ceases, it affects everything around it. For example, human life could not have evolved on Earth without a breathable atmosphere. That was created by plants, which in their turn developed from cells in water.

Can we change things?

Anything that you think, say, or do will have a result, good or bad, even if you cannot see it immediately. We cannot escape from the pattern of cause and effect. Your deeds affect the lives of others, but they also change your own life, by developing habits. A friendly person tends to be one who looks on the bright side of life; someone who is unfriendly is likely to be negative. You gradually shape your own personality by what you think, say and do.

Buddha taught that what you are tomorrow depends on what you do today. This is called *karma* (or *kamma*). Your karma are the actions that you choose to carry out. They are like seeds that produce fruit in the future.

Can we know the future?

Buddhists believe that we shape our future by present actions, but we cannot know the future. As we go through life we are shaped by the results of our actions. This is called 're-becoming.'

By the time we reach the end of our lives, many of our actions are still like seeds, waiting to produce their fruit. Buddhists believe these actions will influence a life in the future. This future life will not be 'you', because Buddhists do not believe in a fixed self, but it will be a life influenced by the results of the one you are living now.

Can we achieve peace?

Buddhists believe that unhappiness is caused by the evils of greed, hatred and ignorance. Those people who succeed in overcoming these evils will achieve a state of happiness and peace that the Buddhists call *nirvana,* in which they are free from all craving.

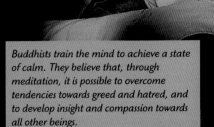

Buddhists train the mind to achieve a state of calm. They believe that, through meditation, it is possible to overcome tendencies towards greed and hatred, and to develop insight and compassion towards all other beings.

DEBATE - Can you shape your own life?

Buddhists think that, if you do something good, you will benefit as a result, whether you are acting for yourself or for someone else. If you do something wrong, even if you are never caught, you change yourself a little by your deed and will suffer the consequences.

So, can you shape your own life?

- No. People are guided from outside by God or by fate.

- Yes. Personal circumstances and choices shape one's life.

How does karma work?

If you are lost and want to find your way, look at a map. Buddhists have the equivalent of a map to show the way that karma affects people's lives. It is called the Wheel of Life.

In the middle of the wheel are three animals: a cock (representing greed), a snake (hatred) and a pig (ignorance). These are shown biting one another's tails, because they feed on one another. Around these there is a circle with

A Tibetan embroidered example of the Wheel of Life, to which everyone is shackled.

people falling downwards or floating upwards: some lives are improving, others declining. Surrounding these are the six realms:

1. At the top is the world of the gods, and of those who like refined, beautiful things.
2. Moving clockwise, the titans are next. They fight against one another.
3. Then there are the animals, content as long as they have their basic needs.
4. The hell realm of those who suffer comes next.
5. Then there are the 'hungry ghosts' – with swords sticking out of their stomachs because they are never satisfied, however much they have.
6. And finally there is the realm of human beings.

These realms represent different ways of living, each with its own problems and opportunities. A Buddha figure appears in each of them, showing people how to improve their lives.

Around the outside of the wheel is a series of images, which shows how karma causes people to move from one realm to another. A blind man, representing ignorance, is followed by a sequence showing how one thing leads on to another. People crave for things, and the craving leads on through their own death to a new life being born, only for the whole sequence to start again.

The wheel keeps turning, through life after life, pushed round by greed, hatred and ignorance. It represents the ordinary world in which we live, which is called *samsara*. It is set within the jaws of a monster, representing death. Buddhists seek to escape from this cycle of behaviour and its consequences. They aim to extinguish the passions caused by greed, hatred and ignorance, so that they may achieve peace and happiness.

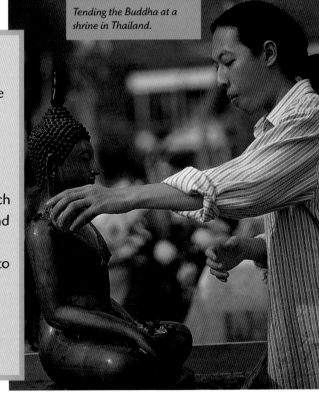

Tending the Buddha at a shrine in Thailand.

The Wheel of Life

The six realms on the Wheel of Life represent different ways of living. Some people seem like animals, and are easily satisfied. Others are always struggling against one another, or are never content. Each realm has its own opportunities and problems, Buddhists say. But it is possible to move from one realm to another. The human realm is the most fortunate of all, as humans can understand the causes of suffering, and overcome them.

How Did Buddhism Start?

The founder of Buddhism was an Indian prince who gave up everything to seek out the truth about life. He found that the biggest problem was suffering, and the way to overcome it was through 'enlightenment'.

SIDDHARTHA GAUTAMA WAS born in Lumbini, northern India, in 563 BCE. He was the son of a local ruler of the Shakya clan, and is sometimes called Shakyamuni (wise man of the Shakyas). Described as a prince, he grew up in comfort, mixing with the other ruling families. He was trained in the arts, was good at sport and seemed destined to rule. He married a local princess, Yasodhara, and together they had a son, Rahula.

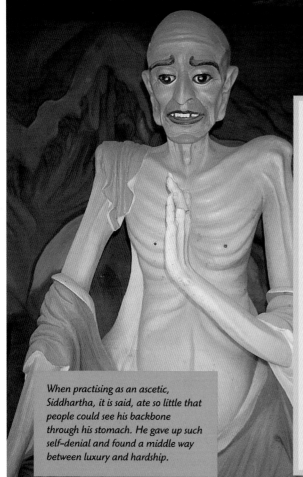

When practising as an ascetic, Siddhartha, it is said, ate so little that people could see his backbone through his stomach. He gave up such self-denial and found a middle way between luxury and hardship.

DEBATE – Can you be religious at home?

Siddhartha left his home and family to lead a solitary and wandering life, seeking an answer to life's problems. In India at that time, that was not an unusual thing to do.

So, is it possible to be religious at home?

* Yes. Family life offers opportunities to learn the truth about life and religion.
* No. You need to get away from all domestic distractions.

A Buddhist shrine set beneath a pipal tree. Many temples have a bodhi tree (or bo tree) to represent the place where Siddhartha became enlightened.

An answer to suffering?

In India at that time there were many wandering *sadhus* (holy men) who were ascetics. An ascetic is someone who chooses to live simply to gain wisdom. Siddhartha tried this, but gave up after seven years when he felt no nearer to finding the answer to suffering. Determined to discover the truth, he sat beneath a pipal tree and vowed he would not leave that spot until he had found the answer. After a night troubled by temptations, he is said to have become enlightened. The tree under which he sat became known as the bodhi tree, meaning the tree of enlightenment.

What is enlightenment?

Siddhartha is called 'Buddha', which is a title, not a name. It means 'the enlightened one'. It is impossible to know what enlightenment is like without being enlightened. But the Buddha's teachings about change, and about suffering and the path to overcome it, were his attempts to explain to people what it was that he came to understand as he sat beneath that tree.

At Siddhartha's birth, a seer (wise man, or fortune teller) announced that Siddhartha would grow up to be either a great ruler or religious leader. His parents kept him from witnessing suffering, in the hope that he would not think about humanity's burdens .

One day, he persuaded his charioteer to take him out of the palace into the streets of the city. There he saw four sights that were to change his life: a sick person, an old person, a corpse and a holy man. Shocked to learn that everyone is liable to sickness, old age, and death, Siddhartha decided that he wanted to leave home and seek an answer to the problem of suffering.

How did the Buddha spread his message?

After his enlightenment, the Buddha went to Sarnath, an ancient holy site. There he met his fellow ascetics, who had deserted him when he gave up his strict discipline. They accepted his new teaching and became his first followers. This is called 'the first turning of the wheel of the Dharma'.

The Buddha spent the next 40 years travelling around northern India teaching and organizing his followers, who went out to spread his teachings further. In India at that time, wandering teachers were largely supported by householders, who would give them food and shelter, so the Buddha was able to travel and teach. He often stayed just outside a town, so that people would come out to hear him.

What kinds of people followed the Buddha?

A wide variety of people came to the Buddha. Some were householders, who generally came with a particular problem or question. Sometimes he was visited by the wealthy, including those with whom he would have mixed when he lived as a prince. Others were ascetics who, like him, had chosen the homeless, wandering life.

The Buddha always tried to make his teaching relevant to the person he was addressing. He saw no point in debating religious ideas for the sake of it. His aim was to understand and overcome suffering, and his teaching was always directed to that end.

Pilgrims at Sarnath, where the Dharma was first taught and the Buddhist community (or sangha) was born. Bowing down (or prostration) is a way of showing the Buddha commitment and respect.

In Theravada Buddhist countries it is quite usual for young boys to spend time as novice (or trainee) monks. Few will choose to remain monks later in life.

Who became nuns and monks?

Some of those who followed the Buddha gave up family life in order to travel around and spread his teaching. As time went on, wealthy patrons gave land so that the Buddha could have regular places to rest (called *viharas*). This was particularly useful during the rainy season, when travel became difficult. Over time, these resting places became teaching centres, where some of his followers began to live. They were the first monasteries, and the full-time followers of Buddha became monks and nuns. They established rules and regulations for living together, recited the Buddha's teachings and gave advice to those who visited.

DEBATE – Should you accept problems?

The Buddha insisted that people should not run away from life's problems, but look at them clearly and learn from them. When a woman brought him her dead child and asked him to make the child well again, he sent her on a quest to bring him seeds from a house where nobody had ever died. In failing to do so, she learned that death was universal, and so came to terms with her own loss.

So, should you always face the truth?

- No. Truth can be painful. It's sometimes better to dream happily than face the truth.
- Yes. Problems can only be overcome if you face them.

What Is It Like To Be A Buddhist?

In Buddhism there is no god to hand out punishments or rewards. Instead, Buddhists try to create good rather than bad karma. They try to follow general guidelines, called precepts, aiming to produce happiness for themselves and others.

Students enjoy a meal of pizzas containing salami, ham and beef. Is eating meat a temptation to be avoided, or is it reasonable and healthy to do so? Buddhism offers general principles about lifestyle and habits, but leaves people to decide for themselves.

RELIGIONS THAT TEACH belief in God generally have rules for people to follow. There are rewards for those who keep to the rules and punishments for those who do not. But because Buddhists see everything as connected with everything else, they do not believe that fixed rules work. What is right for one person might not be right for another. Buddhists do not generally speak about being good or bad, or right or wrong. They speak about being skilful or unskilful. Things are judged skilful if they promote love and acceptance, unskilful if they promote craving, hatred and ignorance.

The third precept of Buddhism teaches that in a romantic relationship individuals must respect one another's wishes, desires and feelings: neither partner should be selfish.

What are The Five Precepts?

For most Buddhists, there are just five basic guidelines, called precepts:

1 Not taking life (but trying to cultivate loving kindness towards all creatures)
2 Not stealing (but cultivating open-handed generosity towards all)
3 Not behaving wrongly or selfishly in one's way of life, or being greedy (but trying to develop simplicity and contentment in life)
4 Not lying (but being honest with yourself, as well as with others)
5 Not abusing drink and drugs (but keeping the mind clear).

The five precepts are presented as a guide to the sort of wise and skilful behaviour that is likely to lead to happiness. A Buddhist is expected to think about how to apply them to his or her own life, to review how successfully this is being done and to learn from any situations that may have caused suffering or unhappiness. The precepts are a form of spiritual training. Keeping to them is a key part of what it means to be a Buddhist.

On festivals and other special occasions, Buddhists may undertake to follow other precepts as well. Monks and nuns have additional rules and regulations for organizing their lives. They are contained in a special set of writings called the *Vinaya*.

DEBATE – Are rules helpful?

Some religions offer rules and regulations, including food laws. Buddhism offers only general principles, and leaves the decision up to the individual. Some Buddhists are vegetarian; others are not. On the one hand, killing is against the first precept; on the other, people may need meat to stay healthy. Killing an animal yourself is one thing; sharing food offered by a meat–eater is another. So do you need rules?

• Yes. It makes life straightforward; you know when you are doing wrong.
• No. Circumstances change, what is right for one person might be wrong for another.

What is the Noble Eightfold Path?

Siddhartha Gautama had lived both as a wealthy prince and as a poor ascetic. Neither way of life gave him an answer to the world's suffering. He discovered a 'middle way' between these extremes, which he set out in the Noble Eightfold Path. The eight steps are not meant to be taken one after another, but are different aspects of the path that Buddhists follow.

The first two are about understanding and attitude (wisdom):

1   Right understanding (of the Buddha's teachings)
2   Right intention (to follow the path).

The next three are about practical ethics:

3   Right speech (to speak in a gentle, not a harsh way; to be positive, not negative or destructive; to be truthful; to speak with a good purpose, not to gossip)

'Western' Buddhists at a countryside retreat in Scotland. Right speech is the precept aimed at promoting honesty and good relationships between people. The Buddha once said that true friendship was the whole of the Buddhist path.

Respecting others

The Buddha saw one of his followers performing a traditional ritual of bowing to the six directions. He explained to his follower that the six directions represent six kinds of human relationships that deserve respect:

* parent and child
* teacher and student
* husband and wife
* friend and friend
* employer and employee
* religious teacher and follower.

Buddhists are therefore encouraged to take seriously the responsibilities that come with each of those relationships, and to respect other people.

4 Right action (keeping the five precepts)
5 Right livelihood (choosing suitable work)

The final three are about meditation and mental training:

6 Right effort (to encourage positive thoughts and remove negative ones)
7 Right mindfulness (to be aware of everything around you)
8 Right contemplation (to practise meditation).

Buddhists are encouraged to balance these three parts. Without wisdom, you cannot see the need for a path. Without mental training, it is difficult to think about the path in a positive way. Without speaking or acting, you cannot put it into practice

Buddhist worship is all part of following the path. But it is not a separate step, and it does not work by magic. What matters is the intention, the attitude and the qualities that it helps to develop in the person who takes part. Worship contributes to both wisdom and mental training.

How do Buddhists find a balanced life?

Some Buddhists think that we all have a Buddha nature within us, and are capable of expressing it. One way of testing progress in this direction is to think about the traditional Buddhist perfections (paramitars), which express the qualities that a Buddha would show. They are generosity, morality, energy, patience; meditation and wisdom.

Why are there Buddhist monks and nuns?

In the Buddha's time, it was normal for people to leave their ordinary life and spend some time learning from a spiritual teacher. The Buddha's full-time followers started organizing themselves into what became known as the *sangha*. The monks were called *bhikkus*, and the nuns *bhikkunis*. In Theravada and Tibetan Buddhism, it is common for people to enter the monastic sangha, even if for only a short period. When Buddhism arrived in China and Japan, it encountered a culture that was more concerned with family life, so fewer people became monks or nuns.

What does a monk or nun do?

The lives of monks and nuns is based on meditation, study and work. Each day, there are practical jobs to do in the monastery (vihara), and times for study and meditation. Nuns and monks also gather in the shrine for worship, to express their devotion to the Buddha.

DEBATE – Vows for life?

Christian monks or nuns take vows for life. Buddhists think that this is unrealistic, because circumstances and people are always changing. They therefore take vows for a limited period of time, and can then choose whether to continue in the monastery or go back home. If they decide on the latter, they can always re-enter a monastery. So, should vows be for life?

- Yes. It shows your commitment to your belief in the Dharma.

- No. It is not practical. You may feel differently in the future.

Study is an important part of life for monks and nuns. It deepens their own understanding, and so enables them to teach and advise others.

Nuns and monks take a daily walk into a local village or town, carrying bowls. People come out of their houses, bow to one or other member of the sangha and place some food in a bowl. The sangha member then bows in return and moves on. This is called the 'alms round'. Finally, the sangha members return to the monastery to eat what they have been given. It is their main meal of the day, which they take before noon. This may look like begging, but in Buddhist countries it is normal for monks and lay people (those who are not monks or nuns) to help one another. Monks and nuns teach and advise the lay people, and in return the lay people offer them practical gifts, such as food. Giving food to the sangha is also a way of cultivating generosity, so the giver will benefit as well as the sangha that receives the food.

What can monks and nuns own?

Monks and nuns have a limited number of possessions. Apart from their robes, they have a bowl, a needle and cotton, a razor and a net for straining their drinking water. They also have strings of beads, which they count with their fingers, one bead after another, as an aid to concentration.

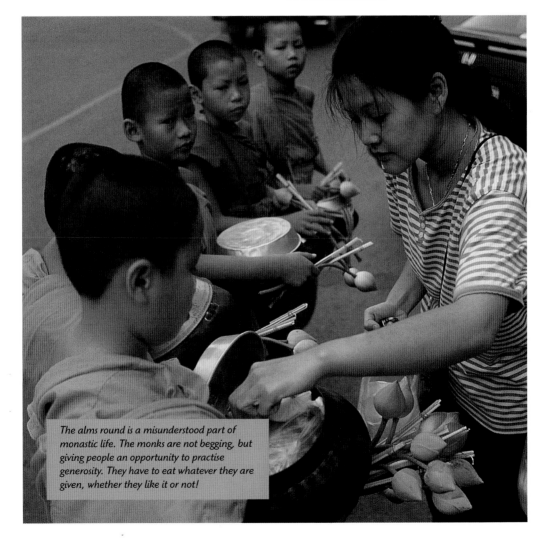

The alms round is a misunderstood part of monastic life. The monks are not begging, but giving people an opportunity to practise generosity. They have to eat whatever they are given, whether they like it or not!

How Do Buddhists Worship?

Many Buddhists think it is helpful to go to a shrine to show respect for the Buddha and to express thanks for his teaching.

UNLIKE OTHER RELIGIONS, Buddhism does not teach belief in a God or gods who have to be worshipped. The Buddha encouraged his followers to think about his teachings, and to accept only those that they understood and found convincing. He taught that people should not put their trust in religious ceremonies or expect them to work as if by magic. What mattered, he said, was not the ceremonies, but the attitude of the people who took part in them.

How do people become Buddhists?

When they have problems, most people look for a refuge. Faced with the truth about suffering and change, those who follow the Buddha think of themselves

Buddhists use religious ceremonies to express and deepen their own thoughts and feelings. What counts are the inner thoughts, feelings and intentions of people who enter a temple, not their actions when they are in the temple.

The Pali Canon is arranged in three parts, and is called the Tipitaka, or 'three baskets'. It includes the teachings of the Buddha, rules for monks and nuns and philosophical writings.

as going for refuge to three things: to the Buddha, to his teachings (Dharma) and to his followers (sangha). They believe that these offer a genuine refuge and way of overcoming suffering.

In a simple ceremony, a person declares that he or she intends to go for refuge to the Buddha, the Dharma and the sangha. This simple act of declaration can be performed as part of a person's regular visit to a shrine or temple for worship (*puja*).

The first time that a person goes for refuge in this way, in the presence of a member of the sangha, is considered the act by which a person becomes a Buddhist. At the same time, the person recites the five precepts that form the basis of the Buddhist way of life.

Do Buddhists read scriptures?

The Buddha did not write his teachings down, but they were passed on by word of mouth for 400 years. The earliest scriptures are the *Pali Canon* (Pali is a language similar to the Buddha's). Later scriptures also claim to be a record of the teachings of the Buddha. One of

Buddhism and other religions

Buddhism is not like other religions. It does not insist on people giving up their existing beliefs. When Buddhists went to China, they found two other religions, Confucianism and Taoism. The Buddhists did not try to displace them, but lived alongside them. To this day, many Chinese take part in both Buddhist and other religious ceremonies. Similarly, when Buddhism arrived in the West, it did not require people to set aside all their existing beliefs – it simply suggested that people should not rely too much on religious separation.

the most famous is the *Lotus Sutra*. Buddhist monks and nuns may study the scriptures, but do not look to them to give them answers to all problems. Buddhists try to think things through for themselves. Zen Buddhists believe that the true teaching of the Buddha has been handed down by word of mouth, and so they do not need to read scriptures.

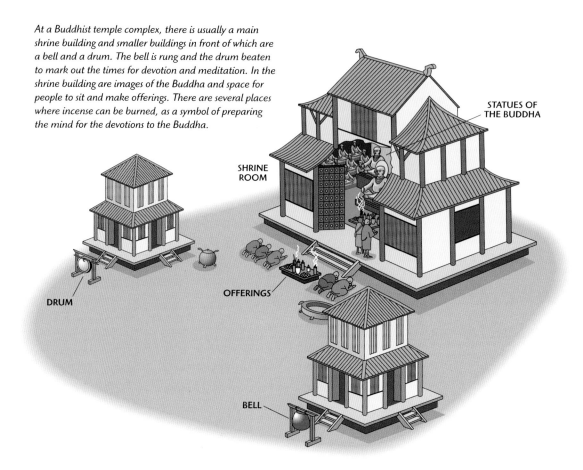

At a Buddhist temple complex, there is usually a main shrine building and smaller buildings in front of which are a bell and a drum. The bell is rung and the drum beaten to mark out the times for devotion and meditation. In the shrine building are images of the Buddha and space for people to sit and make offerings. There are several places where incense can be burned, as a symbol of preparing the mind for the devotions to the Buddha.

STATUES OF THE BUDDHA

SHRINE ROOM

DRUM

OFFERINGS

BELL

Where do Buddhists worship?

There are a wide variety of monasteries, temples and shrines in Buddhist countries. A roadside shrine may have just an image of the Buddha, with space for people to place their offerings. Some temples are huge, with many shrine rooms and different Buddha images. Tibetan temples, in particular, can be very colourful, with large wall-hangings called *thankas*.

Because Buddha is not a god, worship in Buddhist temples is different from worship in other religions. People pay their respects to the Buddha, make offerings and perhaps sit quietly. There will generally be one or more Buddha images called *rupas*, with candles or lamps burning around them and space

for offerings of money or flowers. In front of each image, there will usually be a bowl of sand or rice, into which worshippers can put their burning sticks of incense. In front, there is likely to be an open space for people to sit and meditate, chant or take part in a personal or public ritual. There are often cushions for people to sit on, and in some shrine rooms men sit on one side of the room and women on the other. As well as shrine rooms, a temple will usually have separate rooms where people can meet with the monks and nuns to discuss problems and get advice.

Why do Buddhist places of worship differ?

As Buddhism spread, its forms of worship became influenced by the cultures within which it was practised.

The temples in Japan or China differ from those in India or Thailand. The same basic features are found, but the style of decoration is often quite different. When Buddhism arrived in Tibet, it blended with the older religion of the area, called *Bon*, and adopted some of its traditions. Consequently, Tibetan Buddhist shrines are very colourful and their images strange to Western eyes. By contrast, the Zen tradition in Japan seeks to promote calm meditation and everything is kept very simple.

The simplest form of Buddhist shrine. It consists of an image with space in front where offerings and sticks of incense may be placed.

DEBATE – Elaborate or simple?

Some people love elaborate costumes, images and glimmering candles. Some forms of Buddhism offer this, in the belief that it enables people to engage their emotions and intuition as well as their mind in worship. In other forms, it is thought to be more important to help the mind to become still and alert, and that this can best be achieved by sitting in quiet meditation, in simple surroundings that induce calm.

So, are elaborate rituals helpful?

• Yes. They feed the imagination and people can feel involved in worship.

• No. The mind must be clear, with as few distractions as possible.

The Buddha is not worshipped as a god, so much as a great teacher whose wisdom points the way to personal contentment – nirvana.

Do Buddhists worship at home?

Many Buddhists have a small shrine at home. It may consist of one or more Buddha images (rupas), with perhaps a bowl for incense sticks, candles and some flowers. Tibetan Buddhists in particular like to have a photo of their personal teacher, and this too may be placed on the shrine.

Some Buddhists sit in meditation before their shrine. Others may chant or simply make offerings and put their hands together as a mark of respect for the Buddha. As with other aspects of Buddhism, there are no rules and regulations about the use of shrines at home. People do whatever they find most helpful.

What traditional offerings are made?

It is traditional for Buddhists to make three offerings before an image of the Buddha. Each of them has a special meaning:

1 A candle or lamp – This represents the light of wisdom, overcoming the darkness of ignorance.
2 A flower – Flowers are beautiful, but quickly fade. They are a reminder that everything in life changes.
3 Incense – It is very common to see people lighting sticks of incense and offering them at a shrine. Just as the smell of the incense spreads out in all directions, so Buddhists hope that the benefit of good deeds will spread outward from the person who performs them.

How do Buddhists gain from worship?

If the Buddha taught that people should not rely on religious ceremonies, why do Buddhists perform puja?

People who go to a shrine and make offerings are reminding themselves of the value of following the Buddhist path, and of the qualities that are likely to help them to do so. The person who worships may also feel more calm and focused as a result of the action. However simple the act of devotion, its benefit comes from the inner thoughts and intentions of the person performing it, not from the act itself.

Flowers and human beings, like everything else, change over time. They come into being, blossom and eventually die. Here, Buddhists offer flowers at a shrine as an expression of this belief.

Finding the path

Not to do evil,

To cultivate what is wholesome,

To purify one's mind:

This is the teaching of the Buddha

From the *Dhammapada*, an early Buddhist scripture

For many Buddhists, trying to follow the five moral precepts is their main task. Others would argue that you cannot do so unless you first calm and direct your mind through meditation. Yet others might say that in the first place you need devotion to the Buddha to give you the conviction and determination to follow the Buddhist path.

Making a simple offering before an image of the
Buddha can be an alternative to sitting for hours in
meditation. It helps to direct the mind and expresses
a person's values.

Why do Buddhists meditate?

Buddhists believe that, in order to see
things as they really are, you need to
have a calm and clear mind. Most of the
time, our minds rush from one thing to
another. We may not be aware of what is
happening around us, because we are
too busy planning the future or
remembering the past. The starting
point for meditation is an awareness of
your present surroundings, your
feelings, and the thoughts that are in
your mind. This is the seventh step of
the Noble Eightfold Path.

How do Buddhists meditate?

Most forms of meditation are done
sitting down, in a comfortable but
upright position, to help alertness.
Some Buddhists practise a walking
meditation, very deliberately taking one
step after another, aware of all the
sensations of walking and of the ground
beneath their feet. There are two basic
forms of meditation, called *samatha*
and *vipassana*.

Samatha meditation helps the mind to
become calm and to focus on one thing
at a time. One common form is the
mindfulness of breathing. The person
becomes aware of the breath entering
and leaving the body, and starts by

counting breaths in and out. Gradually, he or she is able to be very still and gently aware of the passage of air in and out of the nostrils. This can produce a state of feeling very alert, yet very calm at the same time. Zen meditation involves sitting with your eyes just slightly open, silently facing a wall. If the mind fills with a rush of images and thoughts, the meditator gently sets them to the one side.

Vipassana meditation helps people to gain insight. A Buddhist may meditate on the fact of change, perhaps by looking calmly at some flowers that are growing old and faded, or even on death. At one time, it was customary for monks to sit and meditate on the stages of decomposition of a corpse! The aim of vipassana is to help a person become fully aware of the reality of life exactly as it is, unclouded by prejudices or dreams.

People sitting silently, in the traditional lotus pose, in a meditation hall. A bell will be rung to mark the different stages in their meditation. Sitting correctly and breathing gently all helps to calm the mind.

Whether or not to meditate

In the West, many people who practise Buddhism find meditation helpful, and some attend classes in meditation even if they are not Buddhists. In some traditional Buddhist countries, people often think that meditation is difficult and best left to the monks. Meditation helps a person to understand his or her mind and the way it works. It does not fill the mind with new ideas, and it is not a form of brainwashing. Some might argue that action is more important. Buddhists might reply that action needs to have direction, and that a calm mind helps to achieve this aim.

What Are The Main Kinds Of Buddhism?

As Buddhism spread eastwards to South-east Asia, northwards to China and Japan and up into the Himalayan countries of Tibet and Nepal, it adapted itself to the needs of the people and cultures in each of those areas.

THERE ARE THREE main branches, or *yanas*, meaning 'vehicles', of Buddhism. They are Theravada Buddhism, which developed in India and South-east Asia, Mahayana Buddhism, which developed in China and Japan, and Vajrayana Buddhism, which developed in northern India and Tibet. All three kinds of Buddhism are now found throughout the world. Some modern Buddhist groups blend teachings and practices from all of these traditional forms.

In Theravada Buddhism monks and lay people help one another. Here, in Sri Lanka, at an open-air Buddhist meeting, monks and lay people exchange ideas and thoughts.

In a Buddhist school, a monk teaches young boys and girls the basics of the faith. As the children grown up, they may spend time on retreat in a monastery, taking time out of their ordinary life to study and think.

Connected with the world

Many Buddhists try to help people in practical ways. This is sometimes called 'engaged Buddhism'. In countries like Sri Lanka, where there has been tension between communities, Buddhists have tried to promote tolerance. They have also established self-help communities to assist rural development. Monks and nuns have to balance work in the community with study, in order to teach and inspire. Political activity by Buddhists shows they do not simply accept suffering, but seek to change what causes it.

What is Theravada Buddhism?

The oldest of the three branches of Buddhism, Theravada Buddhism is probably the closest to the lifestyle and teachings of the historical Buddha. It was originally called the Hinayana, or 'small vehicle', because it was seen as a religion mainly for monks, and narrow in its discipline. Theravada means 'tradition of the elders'.

Monastic life is very important in this tradition. Monks often run schools, so children become used to the idea of being a monk or a nun. Many spend some time in a monastery as a mark of becoming grown-up and able to take responsibility for their own life and religion. Monks and nuns provide not just education, but advice and help for all who ask for it. On some occasions, when they see that society is unfair, the monks may become active politically and campaign for change. This

happened, for example, in Myanmar (previously Burma) in the latter part of the twentieth century. The monks protested and argued for change, using non-violent methods.

What are Theravada scriptures?

The oldest collection of Buddhist scriptures, the Pali Canon, is used by Theravada Buddhists. Each chapter of the first part of these is called a Sutra. This often starts with the words 'Thus have I heard…' and then gives an account of what the Buddha said on a particular occasion when something happened or someone came to him with a particular question.

What is Mahayana Buddhism like?

Buddhism has never tried to impose a particular style of life, but rather to help people discover their own way to put its teachings into practice. When Buddhists arrived in China, they found a society with a strong tradition of family life. There were no homeless religious wanderers, as there were in India in the days of the Buddha. Chinese Buddhism became less concerned with monastic life and more family-based. The religions of Confucianism and Taoism already existed in China, and many people were happy to follow all three religions, without having to choose between them. Far Eastern Buddhism is called Mahayana, meaning 'large vehicle', because it claims that it is suitable for everyone.

Why is devotion to Amida so popular?

Of all the different Buddha images, Amida (or Amitabha) is very popular in the Far East. This Buddha sits in calm meditation, wearing simple robes. Amida is seen as the Buddha of infinite light. There is a tradition that people who call on Amida will, after this life, go to a paradise where conditions are just right to practise the Dharma. Some Buddhists chant the name of Amida as a form of meditation.

What is Zen?

Meditation has always been important for Buddhists. Zen is the Japanese word for meditation, so Zen Buddhism is based on control of the mind. Zen Buddhists practise sitting and walking meditation and also test out their minds with impossible questions, called *koans*.

Zen Buddhists also express the simplicity of meditation through the arts. Temples may have gardens of carefully raked sand and precisely placed rocks and bushes. Zen has inspired painting, calligraphy (decorative writing) and many other activities. It requires a calm waiting for exactly the right moment to do something, or understanding exactly the right line to draw or paint. Zen is based on teachings that are passed on from master to student, and does not rely on scriptures or other written traditions.

Monks stand in rows to chant in this temple in China. Chanting is an alternative to meditation. A familiar phrase repeated over and over again is meant to create a sense of calm and reinforce a positive attitude of mind.

DEBATE - Does devotion bring nirvana?

In the earliest forms of Buddhism, people did not expect to benefit from religious actions, but from their intentions and behaviour. However, some Mahayana Buddhists think Amida Buddha will help them to achieve nirvana if they are devoted to him. They claim devotion shapes their lives. So, does devotion to Amida help?

* Yes. Devotion enables you to enter paradise.

* No. All progress depends on actions and intentions. There are no short cuts.

Two teenagers take refuge through prayer, silence and meditation at Sule Pagoda in Yangon, Burma.

Tibetan Buddhists worship using prayer wheels. Small pieces of paper with mantras (words to be repeated) written on them are then tucked into the wheel. The wheel is swung round on a handle, or turned by the wind or water. Prayer wheels are a reminder that the Dharma works everywhere and through everything.

each with its own special significance. Tibetan monks can be distinguished from their southern counterparts by the colour of their robes, which are deep-red rather than yellow.

What is Tibetan Buddhism?

Buddhism reached Tibet, high in the Himalayas, in about 700 CE, 1 200 years after its beginning. By this time, in northern India, new forms of Buddhism had developed, including Vajrayana, which Buddhist teachers brought to Tibet. 'Vajra' in Vajrayana has two meanings: diamond and thunderbolt. Vajrayana is a form of Buddhism that uses many different methods to help people to achieve enlightenment.

Tibetan Buddhism is colourful and noisy, as people engage their emotions as well as their minds. Processions, dancing and chanting are common at Tibetan festivals. Monks perform a sequence of gestures, called *mudras*,

How did Tibetan Buddhism spread west?

Until the 1950s, Tibet was a very religious country, largely cut off from the rest of the world and ruled by the Dalai Lama and the monks. Then the Chinese invaded and claimed Tibet as part of China. They tried to put an end to Buddhism in Tibet, despite opposition from the Tibetan people. The Dalai Lama fled, and became one of a growing number of exiles living in India. Other senior lamas have also escaped, along with many ordinary Buddhists who want to be free to practise their religion. Consequently, many Tibetan teachers now live in Europe and in the USA. They have taught Tibetan Buddhism to Westerners, and it is now known and practised worldwide.

Who is the Dalai Lama?

The chief teachers in the Tibetan
Buddhist tradition are called lamas,
the most senior of whom is the
Dalai Lama. The present Dalai Lama
is the fourteenth to hold that title.
He lives in northern India, but
travels the world speaking on behalf
of the people of Tibet. When a
lama dies, Tibetan Buddhists believe
that his *karma* will be taken on by
a successor, or *tulku*, who has to be
sought out. They look for a child
who shows signs of being the Dalai
Lama and he is then brought up as
the next Dalai Lama. Each Dalai
Lama is thought to be an
incarnation (human form) of
Avalokiteshvara (the Buddha of
Compassion) because the quality of
Avalokiteshvara's compassion is seen
in and through the lama's life.

*The Dalai Lama speaks at an international
meeting of Buddhists. The Dalai Lama is
believed to be the incarnation of the
enlightened being called Avalokiteshvara.*

What Do Buddhists Celebrate?

Buddhists have no universally agreed ways of marking the big moments in life – birth, coming of age, marriage and death. Each country where Buddhism is practised has developed its own traditions.

IN THERAVADA COUNTRIES, it is usual for Buddhists to marry at a civil ceremony, although they may invite monks to their home to give them a blessing. In Mahayana Buddhism, some temples are registered as places for marriage, and Buddhist monks conduct weddings. Buddhists see marriage as a personal agreement between the partners. If a relationship breaks down, they accept divorce.

When a Buddhist dies, relatives and friends sometimes sit with the body and meditate on the fact of death, and on the qualities of the deceased person.

Buddhist boys become used to monastic life whether as a result of school or by doing a 'rains retreat.'

Buddhists who die are usually cremated, and their ashes put in a monument called a *stupa*. Some stupas, such as those that are claimed to house remains of the Buddha, are huge. Others are small, and often made of wood and can be placed on or near a shrine.

When a Buddhist teacher dies, particularly in the Tibetan tradition, the ashes may be divided between several stupas, each of which is sent to a monastery, or centre, where that teacher had taught.

How do Buddhists mark coming of age?

As a sign of growing up, boys may spend some time in a monastery, living as a monk. Traditionally, this takes place during the rainy season retreat. A boy may first be dressed as a young prince (like Siddhartha), before having his head shaved and putting on monastic robes. Living as a monk for a short time is intended to give young people a sense of discipline. It is a sign that they are now old enough to accept responsibility for themselves. Most of them are happy to return to their ordinary lives after a few weeks.

Can Buddhists be organ donors?

Some Buddhists believe that a new life begins as soon as the person dies. They are therefore happy to allow body organs to be removed for the benefit of other people. Other Buddhists (particularly in the Tibetan tradition) think that a person lingers around his or her old body for some time after death, and removing the organs would disturb the lingering spirit.

An elaborate funeral pyre in Thailand, prepared for the cremation of the mother of a senior monk.

How do Buddhists celebrate New Year?

In Thailand and Burma, New Year is celebrated at the beginning of spring, in April. Water is often used as a symbol of new life. Streams and ponds may dry up in the hot weather, so Buddhists rescue fish and set them free into the rivers. Others free caged birds as a sign of new life. Buddha images are decorated and washed. In Thailand it is quite usual for people to celebrate by having water-fights in the street!

New Year is also a time for celebrating and feasting with families. The festival generally lasts three days. On the third day, people go to the temple to take the 'refuges and precepts' as a way of reaffirming their commitment to the Buddha, to his teaching and to the Buddhist community.

What is Vassa?

In the early days of Buddhism, the Buddha's followers would go out and

One of the traditional ways of celebrating is to eat together. Lay Buddhists sometimes provide food for the monks at festival times or to mark some important event in the life of their family.

Releasing an eel into fresh water is a way of showing compassion towards all living things – part of the Thai celebration of New Year.

about to teach the Dharma. But the rainy season made travelling difficult, so they stayed behind in their resting places to spend time in meditation and study until it was over. This became known as the *rains retreat*.

The tradition continues to this day. Monks and nuns (particularly in the Theravada tradition) usually spend some time each year in retreat. *Vassa* is the celebration that marks the beginning of the rains retreat. It is the time when young men enter the monastic life for a short period. The end of the rainy season is marked by a festival called *Kathina*. Then, lay Buddhists come and present gifts to the monks, to help them live through another year. These gifts might be robes, food or things for use in the monastery.

Celebrating the Buddha's life

Wesak, the festival that celebrates the birth, enlightenment and death of the Buddha is held in April or May. It is the most important festival in Theravada Buddhism. Light is a symbol of enlightenment, so the celebrations include lights and processions with lanterns. People share food and gather to hear talks from the monks. Some Buddhists take extra vows for the day to gain extra merit. It is a time for generosity, and in some parts of the Buddhist world blood donor sessions are held in temple grounds as an example of this.

What is the O-bon festival?

The Buddhist Wheel of Life includes the realm of the 'hungry ghosts', or spirits. Can a hungry spirit be fed, so that it no longer suffers from the pangs of longing? In Japanese Buddhism there is a tradition that, if you feed the monks at the end of a rains retreat, you can save a 'hungry spirit' and release it from the realm where it is trapped.

The O-bon festival, which is held in July, originated from this tradition. Candles and lamps are lit to welcome those who have died. For Japanese Buddhists it is a special family holiday, when families remember their ancestors and especially those who died recently. People often go home to their families for the festival. They may visit the places where their dead relatives lived, or where they died or were cremated. Buddhist priests are invited into the home to recite from the scriptures, and offerings are made at the shrine in the home.

Tibetan monks creating a mandala out of grains of coloured sand. The mandala represents the universe. Disposing of the sands is a symbolic action, showing that nothing is permanent.

How do Tibetan Buddhists celebrate?

As well as celebrating the major Buddhist festivals, Tibetan Buddhists celebrate the birthdays of their major teachers. Sometimes, to prepare a temple for a festival, they put up huge wall hangings (*thankas*) on the outside temple walls for all to see. (Usually, thankas are found on the inner walls of temples and shrines.) They may make huge Buddha sculptures out of butter. As the butter melts away, it is a reminder that everything changes.

Buddhist monks may create circular patterns, called *mandalas*, out of coloured sands. After all the work, the sand is thrown away, and often tipped into a stream. The lesson here is that one should be prepared to create something beautiful and then let it go. The value is in the making, not in trying to hold on to the finished product.

Tibetan festivals include processions of people in colourful costumes, accompanied by the blowing of horns. The celebrations often use dance and drama to help express different aspects of Buddhist teaching.

This lively procession is part of the celebrations for the opening of a Buddhist monastery in Mongolia. Mongolian Buddhists follow the Vajrayana tradition.

Different traditions, similar aims

There are many forms of Buddhism, from the orderly life of monks in South-east Asia to the simplicity of Zen. Different Buddhist groups accept each other's traditions, because different practices suit different people. The general principle is that, whatever helps to overcome greed, hatred and ignorance, and to develop wisdom and compassion, is right for that person.

What Has Buddhism To Say About The World Today?

Buddhism has gained widespread appeal from East to West because it addresses many of the issues that face people in the world today – from war and peace to hunger and health and alcohol and drug abuse.

Rescue workers pick their way through the remains of the World Trade Center in New York, destroyed by terrorists in 2001. Buddhists oppose all violence and killing, because both violate the First Precept, and they point out that hatred is one of the three poisons that keep people trapped in the cycle of suffering.

Can Buddhists approve of killing?

Not taking life is the first and most basic of the Buddhist precepts. Buddhists seek to avoid killing of any sort, but especially the killing of other people. One Japanese Buddhist group, horrified by the death and suffering on both sides caused by the Second World War, and by the atomic bombs dropped on Hiroshima and Nagasaki, is dedicated to bringing about world peace. The group is called Nipponzan Myohoji, and

Taking recreational drugs runs counter to Buddhist teaching because drugs of this kind cloud the mind.

throughout the world its members build peace pagodas to symbolize Buddhism's quest for peace.

What about drugs?

The last of the five Buddhist precepts is about keeping the mind clear and not clouding it with drink or drugs. People under the influence of drugs are not fully aware of the world around them, and may behave foolishly. The same is true of someone who is drunk.

Buddhists do not say that alcohol or drugs are wrong in themselves – after all, drugs are an important part of medical treatment. Rather, it is the abuse of these things, in a deliberate attempt to cloud the mind, that is seen as unskilful. To a Buddhist, trying to escape from reality through drugs is impossible, and can only lead to more suffering. Other things too can drug the mind, such as an

DEBATE – Should you be vegetarian?

Most Buddhists say that it is ideal to be vegetarian, because it avoids killing animals for food. But some people are told they need to include animal protein in their diet or they may be in danger of making themselves ill. The Dalai Lama, for example, was told he should give up his strictly vegetarian diet. He now eats meat for some of the time. Other people cannot grow enough food to stay alive, and without killing animals they would starve.

So, should you eat animal flesh to stay healthy?

• No. It is always wrong to take life, even if you suffer as a result.

• Yes. Because starving or becoming ill is just as destructive as killing animals.

obsession with computer games or some other activity. Anything that takes over your life so that you can scarcely think about other matters would count as a drug. So even something that is perfectly legal would, under such circumstances, be thought of as 'unskilful'.

What is your ambition?

Everyone has some particular goal or ambition. Young people, in particular, often identify with stars of the music world or sporting heroes. They may aspire to be rich and lead a celebrity lifestyle like their idols. Buddhism offers an alternative set of images.

Buddhism recognizes that no two people are alike. These differences are illustrated in the variety of images found in Buddhist shrines and temples. Many of them depict *Bodhisattvas* (enlightened beings), each of whom expresses a particular quality. For example, the Bodhisattva Manjushri represents wisdom. He is shown as a prince, wielding the sword of wisdom in one

hand and holding a book in the other. Students at school or college wishing to clear their thoughts to solve a problem may turn to him for inspiration. Other people might have a need to develop a sense of generosity, or determination. For each of these qualities, there is a particular Buddha image.

If you want to be a great musician, you need to listen to music and watch performers. You see them, and imagine yourself playing or singing in the same way. They inspire you to try to be like them. Similarly, Buddhists meditate on one or other of the Buddha images to develop a particular quality. This is not seen as a selfish ambition, because selfishness is a hindrance to progress,

Outdoor pursuits can be excellent opportunities to develop such qualities as patience, calmness and care of the environment.

Many youngsters aspire to be rich and famous. It is good to have ambitions, but these should be tempered with a sense of wellbeing and realism.

Choosing a career

In choosing a career, Buddhists try to follow the principle of 'right livelihood', the fifth step of the Noble Eightfold Path. This means that your work should not require you to break the Buddhist precepts. For example, it would be difficult for a Buddhist to work as a soldier, butcher or wine merchant, or in any business whose sole aim is to make huge profits. Any work that involves deception, or the exploitation of people for profit, would also involve breaking the precepts. On the other hand, helping the poor, teaching, or providing for people's needs can present a Buddhist with opportunities to develop positive qualities. Work then becomes part of the Buddhist path.

and the very opposite of what the images express. Different people have different ambitions, so there is no one Buddha image that expresses everything that a person can become. Buddhists choose the one that best suits how they see themselves and their lives.

Are men and women equal?

In the Buddha's day, while men sometimes left home to follow the spiritual path as a wandering holy man, women were expected to stay at home and care for a family. But the Buddha said that men and women were equally capable of following the Buddhist path, and of becoming enlightened. Women, he said, could become *anagarikas* (homeless ones) or *bhikkunis* (nuns).

What about abortion and contraception?

Buddhists believe that from the moment a child is conceived it has consciousness in some form, which it receives from earlier lives. They also see human life as a precious opportunity. For these reasons, Buddhists regard abortion as a very serious matter, as it goes against the first precept. For many Buddhists, abortion is only right if the life of the mother is in danger. But contraception is generally welcomed, since over-population can lead to poverty and suffering.

What about the environment?

Buddha taught that everything arises because of causes and conditions: that nothing can exist independently of anything else; that everything is connected with everything else. This was a remarkably scientific way of looking at things for its time, considering that it was put forward some 2 500 years ago.

Thus, Buddhists see human beings as part of a single, ever-changing stream of life, of which the environment is also part. Within this environment, they seek

The world conference on religion and the environment, held in Thailand. It was organized by Buddhists and included representatives of many world religions. Wildlife conservation, pollution and related environmental issues were discussed.

Human error and accidents can cause disaster to the natural environment. Oil can kill sea birds and ruin beaches and coastal habitats. Buddhists recognize that we have a responsibility towards all other species and our environment.

to show compassion to all other creatures. Following the law of karma, harm done to the environment is also harm done to oneself.

Is Buddhism scientific?

Scientific thought is based on making observations, testing them out and trying to find theories to explain them. It does not depend on authority or tradition, but on reason and experience. In this sense, Buddhism is scientific because the Buddha invited people to explore his teachings, to try them out and to accept them only if they found through their experience that they were true.

DEBATE – Should women become nuns?

Buddha argued that women should be able to become nuns. This was controversial because, at the time, most people expected women to stay at home and bring up a family. So, should a woman leave home and live as a nun?

- Yes. If a man can do it, then so should a woman, if she wants to.

- No. Women are better suited to having children and bringing up a family.

REFERENCE

Buddhism started in India and spread to South-east Asia, northwards to China and Japan, and across the Himalayas into Tibet. In modern times it has spread throughout the world, sometimes carried by Buddhists who have decided to emigrate, and also because people from other cultures have chosen to practise Buddhism.

Most Buddhists still live in the traditional Buddhist countries of India, South-east Asia and the Far East. It spread only gradually, and people were free to follow some of their traditional religious ceremonies alongside the new Buddhist ideas. Each form of Buddhism developed to suit the society of that part of the world.

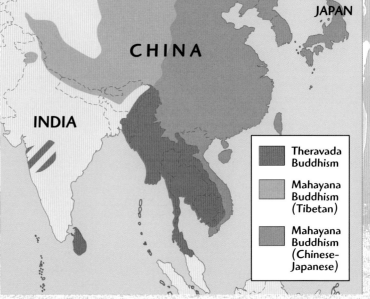

Theravada Buddhism

Mahayana Buddhism (Tibetan)

Mahayana Buddhism (Chinese-Japanese)

Timeline of Buddhism

563–483 bce Siddhartha Gautama (the Buddha)
480 bce First council of monks meets to recite Buddha's teachings
380 bce Second council of monks agrees the rules for monastic life
273 bce The Emperor Asoka, ruler of much of India, becomes Buddhist
c.250 bce A third council of monks agrees the scriptures to be included
    in the Pali Canon
240 bce Asoka's son, Mahinda, takes Buddhism to Sri Lanka
1st century bce First written scriptures (The Pali Canon)
4th century ce Buddhism spreads through China to Korea
6th century Buddhism introduced into Japan
6th century Zen develops from teachings of the Indian monk Bodhidharma
7th century Buddhism introduced into Tibet
12th century Buddhism in India wiped out, mainly through persecution
    by Muslim invaders
17th century Dalai Lamas rule Tibet
20th century   Buddhism spreads to the Western world
1951 Chinese invade Tibet
1959 Dalai Lama escapes to India

Calendar and Major Festivals of Buddhism

Buddhists follow the Dharma in many different ways, and religious ceremonies are optional for them. However, most Buddhists take part in festivals during the year to celebrate particular events and traditions. In particular, festivals offer a chance for them to gather to hear talks on the teachings of the Buddha, to take part in worship, and to strengthen their commitment to the Buddhist way of life. The most important festival of the year is Wesak, which is celebrated by a majority of Buddhists.

New Year (April in Burma and Thailand; January in Japan)
Wesak – birth, enlightenment and death of the Buddha (April/May)
O-bon – for the 'hungry ghosts' (in Japan) July
Asala – first preaching of the Buddha (July/August)
Vassa – start of the 'rains' retreat (follows Asala)
Kathina – end of the 'rains' retreat (October/November)
(Festivals and dates vary between the three main branches of Buddhism. There are a large number of lesser festivals, especially within Tibetan Buddhism.)

The Six Major Faiths

BUDDHISM
Founded
535 BCE in Northern India

Number of followers
Estimated at 360 million

Holy Places
Bodh Gaya, Sarnath, both in northern
India

Holy Books
Tripitaka

Holy Symbol
Eight-spoked wheel

JUDAISM
Founded
In what is now Israel, around 2000 BCE

Number of followers
Around 13 million religious Jews

Holy Places
Jerusalem, especially the Western Wall

Holy Books
The Torah

Holy Symbol
Seven-branched menorah (candle stand)

CHRISTIANITY
Founded
Around 30 CE, Jerusalem

Number of followers
Just under 2 000 million

Holy Places
Jerusalem and other sites associated
with the life of Jesus

Holy Books
The Bible (Old and New Testaments)

Holy Symbol
Cross

HINDUISM
Founded
Developed gradually in prehistoric times

Number of followers
Around 750 million

Holy Places
River Ganges, especially at Varanasi
(Benares). Several other places in India

Holy Books
Vedas, Upanishads, Mahabharata,
Ramayana

Holy Symbol
Aum

SIKHISM
Founded Northwest India, 15th century CE

Number of followers 22.8 million

Holy Places
There are five important, takhts, or seats of high authority: in Amritsar, Patna Sahib, Anandpur Sahib, Nanded and Talwandi.

Sacred Scripture
The Guru Granth Sahib

Holy Symbol
The Khanda, the symbol of the Khalsa.

ISLAM
Founded
610 CE in Arabia (modern Saudi Arabia).

Number of followers
Over 1 000 million

Holy Places
Makkah and Madinah, in Saudi Arabia

Holy Books
The Qur'an

Holy Symbol
Crescent and star

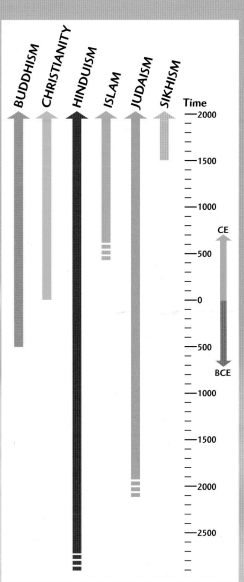

While some faiths can point to a definite time and person for their origin, others cannot. For example, Muslims teach that the beliefs of Islam predate Muhammad and go back to the beginning of the world. Hinduism apparently developed from several different prehistoric religious traditions.

GLOSSARY

Alms Offerings of food and other things, given to Buddhist monks.

Ascetic Someone who has chosen to live a life of strict discipline and self-denial for religious reasons.

Bhikkhu A Buddhist monk.

Bhikkuni A Buddhist nun.

Buddha Title given to Siddhartha, meaning 'the enlightened one'.

Dharma The teaching of the Buddha.

Dukkha Suffering.

Enlightenment A state of perfect understanding, in which a person sees things exactly as they are.

Karma (kamma) Actions that promote results after the event.

Koan A question to which there is no apparent logical answer, often used in Zen mental training.

Lama A senior teacher in the Tibetan Buddhist tradition.

Lay person Someone who has not been ordained as a monk or nun; an ordinary member of society.

Mahayana Buddhism The form of Buddhism that developed particularly in the Far East, and emphasized that it was suitable for all, not just for monks and nuns.

Mandala A special pattern, often made with coloured sand, particularly at festival times.

Mantra Short phrases that people chant over and over.

Meditation Calming and training of the human mind.

Monastic life The life of monks and nuns, following the special rules that are known to Buddhists as the Vinaya.

Nirvana A state of peace, free from greed, hatred and ignorance.

Pagoda A memorial containing relics of the Buddha or one of his followers, known originally as a stupa, it may also be called a dagoba, or a chorten. It may also be used for the whole temple complex, particularly in Burma.

Paramitars Qualities that Buddhists seek to cultivate.

Pilgrim Someone who travels to a holy place to express their commitment to their religion.

Poisons, the Three These are: greed, hatred and ignorance.

Precepts Moral guidelines for following the Buddhist path.

Puja Worship; devotion to the Buddha.

Re-becoming The Buddhist teaching that people are always changing, depending on their karma. This is also believed to continue when one life ends and then influences another which is about to start.

Refuge A place of security; Buddhists claim to go for refuge to the Buddha, his teachings and his followers.

Reincarnation The popular idea in Indian religious thought that people have a soul that can pass from one body to another; this is often mistaken for Buddhist belief. (Buddhists believe that there is no permanent soul to pass on, but that lives influence one another through their karma.)

Retreat The opportunity to take time away from the routine of life for reflection and study.

Rupa An image of the Buddha, often used in worship.

Sadhu The traditional title for a holy man in India.

Samatha Meditation that leads to calmness of mind.

Samsara This world of constant change that we inhabit, influenced by greed, hatred and ignorance.

Sangha The community of the Buddha's followers, both monastic and lay.

Scriptures Writings that are regarded as sacred to a particular religion, treated with respect, and used for guidance.

Shakyamuni (wise man of the Shakya clan.) A title for the historical Buddha.

Shrine A place of worship, having one or more Buddha images. It is sometimes the whole temple building or a room used to house Buddha images.

Skilful means Knowing the right thing to do in a situation, without needing to follow rules.

Stupa A monument, containing the physical remains of the Buddha or one of his followers.

Sutra The name given to chapters of the Buddhist scriptures; it literally means 'thread', since it gives the 'thread' of a debate or argument.

Thanka A wall hanging, used especially in Tibetan Buddhism.

Theravada Buddhism The branch of Buddhism that developed in India and then spread through South-east Asia; probably the earliest of the existing forms of Buddhism.

Tulku A child who is believed to be born with the karma of a senior lama (popularly described as a reincarnation of that lama).

Vajrayana Buddhism The form of Buddhism found mainly in Tibet and the surrounding area.

Vinaya Rules for monks and nuns.

Vipassana Meditation leading to insight into the truth of life.

Wheel of Life Image which shows the Buddhist view of the constantly changing world, including the different realms of existence and the links which illustrate how karma works.

Zen The Japanese word for meditation; a form of Buddhism based on meditation.

FURTHER INFORMATION

BOOKS TO READ

For large-format illustrated books on Buddhism, try:

Buddhism: the illustrated guide, ed. Kevin Trainer, Duncan Baird Publications, 2001

The Vision of the Buddha, Tom Lowenstein, Duncan Baird Publications, 1996

Buddhism, Pushpesh Pant, Tiger Books International, London, 1997

Living Buddhism, Andrew Powell (with a foreword by the Dalai Lama), British Museum Press, 1989

Of the many school textbooks on Buddhism, two are by the author of this present book, and take further the ideas that are outlined here. They are:

The Buddhist Experience, Hodder & Stoughton, 2nd edition, 2000

Buddhism: a new approach (written with Steve Clarke), Hodder & Stoughton, 1996

The Buddhist Experience (Foundation Edition) Jan Thompson, Hodder & Stoughton, 2000, offers a simplified version of the main textbook.

The best-loved collection of the Buddha's teachings, and probably the oldest, is the Dhammapada (which translates as 'the path of the teaching'). Its short sayings give a sense of the Buddha's teachings, and of the Buddhist way of life. It is available in many different translations.

Three adult books that are written in a very straightforward way, and give a good idea about the beliefs of modern Buddhists:

Teach Yourself: Buddhism, Clive Erricker, Hodder & Stoughton, 1995.

Buddhism Without Beliefs, Stephen Batchelor, Bloomsbury, 1998, offers a modern, relevant introduction to the Buddhist path.

The Miracle of Mindfulness, Thich Nhat Hanh , Rider, 1991, was originally written in 1976. It is a wonderful book for giving an idea of the way Buddhists train the mind to be aware of everything and to enjoy every moment.

Of the many books written by the Dalai Lama, try:

Ancient Wisdom, Modern World: Ethics for the New Millennium, Little Brown & Co, 1999

For college students and teachers:

Buddhism: a Student's Approach to World Religions, Denise Cush, Hodder & Stoughton, 1994.

An Introduction to Buddhism, P Harvey, CUP, 1990.

Mahayana Buddhism, P Williams, Routledge, 1989

What the Buddha Taught, Walpola Rahula, Oneworld Publications (re-issued, but originally written in 1959)

An Introduction to Buddhist Ethics, P Harvey, CUP, 2000

WEBSITES

BuddhaNet
This site (www.buddhanet.net) gives a wonderful range of study materials from basic introductions to illustrations of Buddhist art. It covers all the main branches of Buddhism, and presents Buddhist teachings in a particularly accessible and straightforward way. It includes an on-line magazine, and teaching materials for all age groups.

ORGANIZATIONS

www.ciolek.com/WWWVL-Buddhism.html
This site keeps track of leading information facilities in the fields of Buddhism and Buddhist studies

London Buddhist Society
58 Eccleston Square
London SW1
Tel: (020) 7834 5858

The Society represents all branches of Buddhism, and provides information about Buddhist groups throughout the UK.

A major centre for the Theravada tradition in the UK:
Amaravati Buddhist Monastery
Great Gaddesden
Hemel Hempstead
Hertfordshire HP1 3BZ
Tel: (01442) 842455

INDEX

8/17

Southborough Library
Southborough Lane
Bromley BR2 8HP
020 8467 0355

Southborough Library
0208 467 0355
https://capitadiscovery.co.uk/bromley
In partnership with

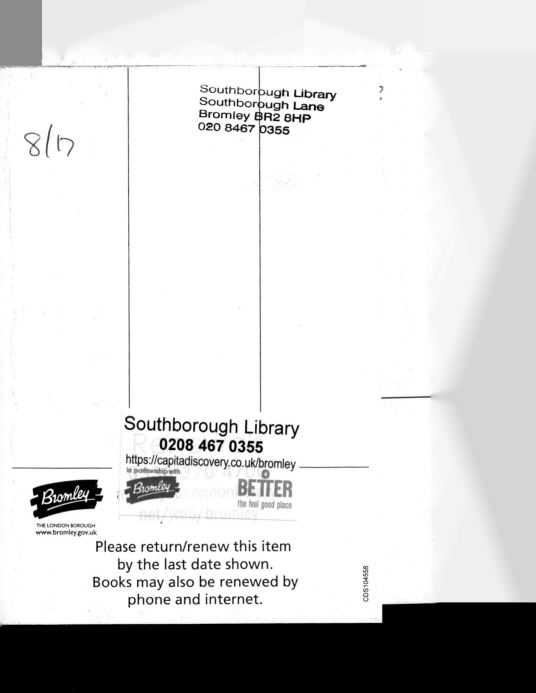

BETTER
the feel good place

THE LONDON BOROUGH
www.bromley.gov.uk

Please return/renew this item
by the last date shown.
Books may also be renewed by
phone and internet.

CDS104558

100

things you should know about

NOCTURNAL
ANIMALS

100

things you should know about

NOCTURNAL
ANIMALS

Camilla de la Bedoyere

Consultant: Steve Parker

First published as hardback in 2008 by Miles Kelly Publishing Ltd
Bardfield Centre, Great Bardfield, Essex, CM7 4SL

Copyright © Miles Kelly Publishing Ltd 2008

This edition published 2009

2 4 6 8 10 9 7 5 3 1

Editorial Director: Belinda Gallagher
Art Director: Jo Brewer
Assistant Editor: Carly Blake
Volume Designers: Sally Boothroyd, Jo Brewer
Image Manager: Lorraine King
Indexer: Gill Lee
Production Manager: Elizabeth Brunwin
Reprographics: Anthony Cambray, Ian Paulyn
Archive Manager: Jennifer Hunt
Editions Manager: Bethan Ellish
Editions Assistant: Toby Tippen

ISBN 978-1-84810-099-2

Printed in China

British Library Cataloguing-in-Publication Data
A catalogue record for this book is available from the British Library

ACKNOWLEDGEMENTS
The publishers would like to thank the following artists who have contributed to this book:
Mike Foster, Ian Jackson, Mike Saunders
Cover artwork: Ian Jackson
All other artworks from the Miles Kelly Artwork Bank

The publishers would like to thank the following sources for the use of their photographs:
Page 6 Frans Lanting/Frans Lanting PL/FLPA; 8 Tui de Roy/Minden Pictures/FLPA;
9(t) S D K Maslowski/FLPA, (c) Terry Whittaker/FLPA; 11 Kevin Schafer/Corbis; 12(b) Frans Lanting/FLPA;
13(b) NHPA/Martin Harvey; 14 Mark Jones/Oxford Scientific; 15(t) EcoView/Fotolia.com,
(b) Joel Sartore/National Geographic/Getty; 16 Tui de Roy/Minden Pictures/FLPA;
19 Audrey Eun/Fotolia.com; 20(t) Oxford Scientific, (b) Satoshi Kuribayashi/Oxford Scientific;
22 Cosi/Fotolia.com, (t) Roger Wilmshurst/FLPA, (b) David Cayless/Oxford Scientific;
23 Don Brown/Animals Animals/Earth Scenes/Photolibrary; 24 Fred Bavendam/Minden Pictures/FLPA;
26 Marian Bacon/Animals Animals/Earth Scenes/Photolibrary; 32 Jurgen & Christine Sohns/FLPA;
33(t) BIOS - Auters Watts Dave/Still Pictures, (b) Professor Jack Dermid/Oxford Scientific;
35 Mitsuaki Iwago/Minden Pictures/FLPA; 38(c) Animals Animals/Earth Scenes/Photolibrary;
39 Tim Shepherd/Photolibrary; 40 NHPA/Simon Booth; 41(b) Michael Quinton/Minden Pictures/FLPA;
42 Martin Dohrn/naturepl.com; 43 Deco/Alamy; 44 NHPA/Martin Harvey;
45(t) Malcolm Schuyl/FLPA, (b) Frans Lanting/FLPA; 47 Derek Middleton/FLPA

All other photographs are from:
Corel, digitalSTOCK, digitalvision, iStockphoto.com, John Foxx,
PhotoAlto, PhotoDisc, PhotoEssentials, PhotoPro, Stockbyte

Made with paper from a sustainable forest

www.mileskelly.net   info@mileskelly.net   www.factsforprojects.com

Contents

1 Imagine standing in a forest as the sun goes down. Listen carefully and you will hear animals stirring and moving in the moonlight. Animals that are most active at night are called 'nocturnal'. From bugs to bears and bats to cats, there are thousands of animals that wait for the day to draw to an end and darkness to fall.

▶ The beautiful ocelot comes out at night to look for food. This cat lives in Central and South America and it hunts for birds, rodents, lizards and bats.

Super senses

2 Nocturnal animals are mainly active at night. This means they need super senses to find their way around in the dark. The darkness offers some protection from predators – animals that may want to eat them – but without great senses they would find it hard to search out food and mates.

▼ This maned wolf is sniffing the air trying to pick up the scent of its prey. Dogs' noses, or muzzles, are filled with smell-detecting cells. The black, leathery end to a dog's nose has two large nostrils, which pass the scents, or odours, over the smell-detecting cells.

3 The five main senses are sight, hearing, smell, touch and taste. Nocturnal animals usually have several or all of their senses heightened. These super senses are what help them to survive.

4 Members of the dog family have an incredible sense of smell. Some of them can detect odours, or smells, up to 50 times better than a human can. Wild dogs, such as wolves, coyotes, foxes and jackals, hunt at night. They use their large sensitive noses, or muzzles, to help them find their prey.

5 Raccoons not only have good eyesight for seeing in the dark, they have sensitive fingertips, too. These mischievous animals paddle in water, feeling under rocks for hiding crayfish, a type of shellfish. They use their long, agile fingers to grab the crunchy creatures before cracking them open to eat.

▲ This smart raccoon knows that it may find some eggs or chicks inside a bird's nesting box.

▲ A Malayan tapir is hard to see in the dark. It feeds on twigs and leaves in the forest.

6 Nocturnal animals may have super senses, but some of them have an extra trick to help them stay hidden from view — camouflage. Dull colours and dappled patterns on their skin or fur help them blend in with their surroundings. Malayan tapirs have distinctive coat patterns with black fur at the front and white at the back. This breaks up their outline and fools tigers – their main predators.

THE TOUCHY-FEELY GAME

Play this game to find out just how useful a sense of touch is.

You will need:
Two pillow cases
Small objects with different textures
(rough, smooth, cold, furry, etc)
A friend

1. Each person must secretly place five objects in their pillow case.
2. Swap pillow cases with your friend.
3. Use your fingers to feel each object and work out what it is. No peeking though!

Bright eyes

7 **Finding your way in the dark is much easier if you can see well.** Human night vision isn't very good and we find it hard to see anything in much detail without light to help us. Many nocturnal animals have astonishing vision and they can see a world of activity that's invisible to us.

8 **Most snakes rely on their senses of smell, hearing or touch to detect prey, but nocturnal tree snakes rely on their vision, too.** They have narrow faces that allow them to clearly see what's right in front of them. Once a tree snake has spotted its prey, it folds its neck into an S-shape, focuses its eyes and then lunges with lightning speed. Its vision is so sharp, a tree snake can judge the distance to its prey with amazing, deadly accuracy.

▲ A tawny owl can spot tiny prey, such as mice, with ease. Its mottled feathers and dull colours help it to remain hidden as it hunts.

▲ Vine snakes live in trees where they hunt their prey, such as lizards or passing birds. Their bodies are long and extremely slender and they have extremely good eyesight.

9 Tarsiers are odd-looking nocturnal animals that live in the tropical rainforests of Southeast Asia. They have enormous eyes and each eyeball is bigger than the animal's brain! Tarsiers can't move their eyes but they can swivel their heads 180 degrees in each direction, which helps them to hunt insects at night.

◄ Tarsiers dart around the treetops in their forest home. As well as having amazing vision, they have good hearing, too.

Light
Pupil narrows

10 Cats are well-known for their night-time hunting skills and owe much of their success to their eyesight. They have large eyes that are especially good at helping them to see at night. The pupil of each eye – the black part in the centre – can open up wide to let in more light in dim conditions. The back of the eyeball is coated in a mirror-like layer, which reflects light, making vision even clearer.

Darkness
Pupil opens wide

▲ The pupils of cats' eyes narrow and widen according to the amount of light there is.

I DON'T BELIEVE IT!

Mammals are furry animals and have been around for more than 200 million years. Most were nocturnal until the dinosaurs died out 65 million years ago. With their major predators gone, mammals were finally able to come out in daylight!

11 In an animal's eyes there are two types of cell that help them to see – rods and cones. Rods help eyes to detect light and cones help eyes detect colour. Nocturnal animals are usually colour blind. This is because they have a large number of rods in their eyes, which means there isn't much room left for the colour-detecting cones.

Noises in the dark

12 **Animals need to communicate with each other, and many do this by making noises.** Communicating by sound is especially important to nocturnal creatures as noises carry well at night – a time when vision is not always so useful.

13 **In the wild, night is not a quiet, peaceful time.** The air can be filled with the screeching of owls, booming roars of lions and endless chatter of cicadas and grasshoppers. Animals that live in groups are described as being 'sociable', and nocturnal creatures use a variety of sounds to communicate. Some sounds are made using voices, while others are made by foot stomping and drumming.

◄ Grasshoppers have 'ears' on their legs or bodies rather than their heads. Males rub their wings or legs together to make noises.

▼ A lioness roars loudly to scare predators away from her cubs. Lions prefer to hunt in the cool of night.

14

At night, white-tailed deer are on their guard for predators that may be lurking nearby. If they sense danger, the deer use sound to alert their herd. They make snorting noises through their noses and beat the ground with their hooves. Foot-stomping may help to scare predators away, too.

15

Crocodiles and alligators are impressive night-time hunters. They rest in the day, soaking up the sun. At night they become quick-moving creatures whose roars carry far across the still water. Male alligators make loud booming calls to attract females in the dark, but it's also been discovered that they can make rumbling low sounds that we can't hear.

▶ Bat-eared foxes have huge ears. They mostly eat insects and use their amazing sense of hearing to listen for beetle larvae gnawing through dung balls.

▲ A threatened crocodile hisses, bellows and roars before attacking.

16

Many nocturnal creatures have good hearing. Some have developed very large ears, or ears that can be moved to pinpoint noises better. Sound is 'caught' by the outer ear and then channelled through the ear canal to the hearing organ – the cochlea – inside the head. Sound information is then carried to the brain as electrical messages.

17 Many animals rely on their sense of smell far more than humans do and this is especially true of nocturnal animals. They use their sense of smell to find food, detect predators and find out about the other animals that are in their habitat – animals that may be hidden from view in the darkness.

Brain Teaser

A hungry sloth bear digs up 100 termites in one nest. In the next nest, he gets double that number. In the third nest he greedily gobbles up only half of the original number.

How many termites did the sloth bear eat altogether?

Answer: 350

▲ Kiwis tap the ground with their sensitive beaks to disturb worms and insects. They capture their prey by pushing their beaks into the soil. They also eat snails, spiders and berries.

18 Kiwis are rare, night-active birds from New Zealand and they have the best sense of smell of any bird. These fluffy birds have nostrils at the tips of their beaks and they use them to sniff out worms and other insects in leaf litter. Their eyesight is very poor, but they can hear well.

19 Snakes can 'taste' smells with their tongues and they rely greatly on scents in the darkness. Snakes are able to smell in two ways – with their nostrils, or with their long, forked tongues. A snake flicks its tongue in the air to pick up scent particles, which are transferred to the roof of its mouth. Messages are sent to its brain that tell the snake about any nearby animals. This is especially useful when hunting at night.

Nostril

Jacobson's organ

◄ ▼ A rat snake flicks its tongue in and out to pick up odours and transfer them to the Jacobson's organ, where they are sensed.

▼ Skunks have poor eyesight and can't see much further than a few metres in front of them. They use their excellent sense of smell to find food in the darkness.

20 Skunks are mostly active at twilight. These black-and-white striped animals spend the day in burrows and come out at sunset to look for food. They have a strong sense of smell and use it to sniff out bugs and small creatures such as mice and frogs. If threatened, a skunk sprays a foul-smelling liquid at its attacker – some say it's like a mixture of of rotten eggs, burnt rubber and garlic!

▼ A sloth bear's sucking noises can be heard up to 100 metres away!

21 By night, shaggy-haired sloth bears shuffle noisily through the forests in India. They hunt for termites and other bugs to eat and they find them using their noses. Once they pick up the scent of an ant or termite nest they rip it open using their long claws and suck up the tasty insects like a vacuum cleaner!

Feeling the way

22 Nocturnal animals often need a good sense of touch because it gives them extra information about their dark surroundings. Whiskers, hairy snouts, delicate fingertips and soft skin – there are many ways that animals can feel what's around them in the dark.

Whisker–like feathers

23 Frogs and toads have very sensitive skins and the natterjack toad is no exception. This nocturnal toad spends the day hiding under rocks and stones. At night it emerges to hunt for insects, spiders and worms. If it's disturbed by a predator, a natterjack toad can lighten or darken the colour of its skin to blend in with its surroundings. This helps it to hide from hungry hunters.

▶ Natterjack toads hunt for food at night. They can lighten or darken their skin colour to hide from enemies.

◀ Kakapos grow to a length of around 64 centimetres and they have small, useless wings. When they walk they hold their bristly faces close to the ground to feel their surroundings. Kakapos only breed every two to four years.

◀ A harvest mouse uses its sensitive whiskers to help find its way in the darkness.

24 Kakapos are the only nocturnal, flightless parrots in the world. Like all birds, they are very sensitive to touch, but kakapos have special whisker-like feathers near their beaks that they use to feel around. These, combined with their well-developed sense of smell, help the birds to find food, such as roots, fruit, nectar and fungi, in the twilight. Kakapos also give off a sweet-smelling body odour that may let other birds know they are there.

25 When a harvest mouse creeps quietly through the shadows, it uses its whiskers to feel the way. Whiskers are long, sensitive hairs. If a mouse pokes its head into a narrow space, it can tell by the pressure on its whiskers whether it can squeeze its whole body through.

26 The brushtail possum has a big, bushy tail that is very sensitive. At night when it becomes active, the possum holds its tail in the air and waves it around to feel its surroundings.

Brushtail possums live in Australia and many live in and around cities and towns. During the day they rest in tree hollows or even in house lofts!

I DON'T BELIEVE IT!

There are less than 90 kakapos alive in the entire world and every one of them has been given its own name. They live on four small islands near New Zealand where a team of scientists work hard to save them from extinction.

Fred

▶ The underside of the brushtail possum's tail is hairless, which helps it grip as it climbs trees.

Night-time bugs

27 **Insects and other bugs are amongst the noisiest nocturnal animals, especially in hot countries.** An evening walk in a rainforest is accompanied by a chorus of clicks, buzzing, humming and chattering. These are some of the sounds made by millions of insects, which are invertebrates – animals without backbones.

▲ Common earwigs are insects that measure 8 to 18 millimetres in length. They are native to Europe, but are found in many countries.

28 **Just like bigger creatures, insects and bugs use sound to communicate with each other at night.** Cockroaches are leathery-skinned insects that are common throughout the world. Most spend their time scuttling silently through the leaf litter and twigs on the forest floor. However, the Madagascan hissing cockraoch can hiss if it's disturbed by pushing air out through its abdomen.

29 **They may look menacing, but earwigs are completely harmless.** By day they hide under leaves or in cracks and crevices. At night they come out to eat rotting plant and animal matter. They have pincers on the ends of their tails, which they use to scare predators away.

◄ Cockroaches can feel movement through their feet, which warns them to dash under cover to avoid predators.

▲ Feathery moth antennae can detect tiny scent particles.

30 **Moths have special organs on the front of their heads called antennae.** These long, slender or feathery structures detect smells and moths use them to find food and mates. These sensitive organs also help moths find their way in the dark. Moths with damaged antennae can't fly in straight lines – they crash into walls or fly backwards!

▲ Female moon moths produce a chemical that tells males they are ready to mate. Males use their antennae to pick up the scent of the female moths from several hundred metres away.

31 **Moths are some of the most elegant and beautiful nocturnal insects.** They have decorative patterns that help to camouflage, or hide, them. Members of the tiger moth family are often brightly coloured to tell predators that they are poisonous. Tiger moths also make high-pitched clicks to deter bats, which hunt by sound not sight. Once a bat has tried to eat one nasty-tasting tiger moth, it knows to avoid all clicking moths!

◀ There are many different types of tiger moth but most of them have fat bodies and brightly coloured wings. These warn predators that they are poisonous.

BED-SHEET BUGS!

Find out what nocturnal insects share your habitat.

You will need:
Large white sheet   torch
notebook and pencil or camera

On a warm evening, hang a sheet up outside and shine a torch onto it. Wait patiently nearby and soon insects will be attracted to the sheet. Take photos or make sketches of all the bugs you see so you can identify them later. Be careful not to touch them though!

Light at night

▶ Click beetles have two bright, glowing spots on their backs and one underneath their abdomen.

32 One way for some nocturnal animals to deal with the dark is to turn on the lights! Some of the most striking nocturnal creatures are fireflies and they light up by a process called bioluminescence (bio-loom-in-ess-ens). All sorts of animals can glow in the dark including insects, spiders, fish and worms.

▼ The flashing lights of fireflies are hard to miss, even in a dark, wet woodland. These beetles are also known as lightning bugs.

33 If you're a small, dull nocturnal insect it can be hard to attract a mate. Fireflies, which are actually a type of beetle, overcome this problem by flashing lights at one another. Tropical fireflies gather together and flash lights at the same time, making a spectacular light show. The lights turn on in patterns that vary according to the type of firefly. It's thought that firefly larvae may also use their lights to warn predators not to eat them.

20

34 Flashlight fish live where sunlight scarcely reaches — in deep water or caves. They have areas under their eyes called 'photophores'. These contain bacteria that produce light. The light helps the fish to see where they are going. It also attracts mates and lures prey in to eat. If a bigger animal comes too close, the fish flicks its light on and off before swimming away.

▲ Flashlight fish use their light to attract shrimps and small fish to eat.

35 Bioluminescence is a chemical process that happens inside an animal's body. Fireflies have special organs on their abdomens that contain these essential chemicals. When they mix with oxygen, a reaction occurs, making a sudden bright flash of light.

I DON'T BELIEVE IT!

Some crafty fireflies flash their lights to grab a bite to eat. They aren't after mates, but they fool other fireflies into thinking that they are. When the curious insect comes to investigate the flashing, they find themselves being attacked — and maybe eaten!

36 Bobtail squids have developed a bright way to forage for food at night and remain invisible to nearby predators. These animals can flash light around themselves, helping to hide their shadows as they swim. This clever trick is achieved with the help of some bioluminescent bacteria and some shiny plates that work like mirrors to reflect the light in lots of directions.

▲ Bobtail squids are small, soft-bodied animals that live in coastal waters, especially around Hawaii.

Coasts and seas

37 In water as on land, some animals choose to stay hidden from view in the daylight hours, but emerge at night. Many sea creatures live in waters so deep that light never reaches them and they live in constant darkness. In shallower water it is bright by day, but as the sun sets, many kinds of fish start their feeding and breeding.

▲ On wet, stormy nights, European eels can survive out of water for several hours.

38 The European eel is an odd-looking fish that can even travel across land. At night these long, snake-like fish may leave the water and slither across damp ground. They do this as they journey back to their breeding grounds to reproduce.

39 Horseshoe crabs are most active at night, mainly to avoid predators. They are called 'living fossils' because they have barely changed in 300 million years. They live in coastal waters but come to land to mate. These unusual animals wait until sunset before marching up onto the beaches where the females dig holes to lay their eggs – often several thousand each!

▶ Horseshoe crabs can reach 60 centimetres in length. They live in North America and Southeast Asia.

▶ Also known as monkfish, angel sharks are heavily fished for food and many types are endangered.

40 Angel sharks are night-time hunters.

Different kinds live all around the world and most grow to one to two metres in length. They were once common in the Atlantic Ocean and Mediterranean Sea, but now some are almost extinct. These flat sharks lie camouflaged on the seafloor during the day. At night, they swim upwards catching small, shelled animals and fish as they go.

▶ With their wide mouths and sharp teeth, moray eels make fearsome predators.

41 Moray eels are nocturnal predators.

They lie in wait for their prey, then ambush it. These long, thick-bodied fish rely on their sense of smell to detect other animals, so they can feed at night just as easily as in the day. They normally hide in cracks and crevices on the sea floor, but will emerge from a hiding place under the cover of darkness.

23

Dark depths

42 As darkness falls in the ocean, the world's biggest octopus comes out to hunt. The giant Pacific octopus can measure an incredible 7.5 metres from one tentacle tip to another. These extraordinary animals have soft, fleshy bodies and eight tentacles that are covered in large suckers.

▼ Ocean-living molluscs such as this giant Pacific octopus don't have hard shells to protect their soft bodies, so they need some impressive tricks to help them survive.

43 During the day, octopuses sleep in dens on the seabed close to land. They forage for food at night, searching for fish and shelled animals to eat. They kill their prey by biting it or pulling it apart with their tentacles. Sometimes, octopuses pour poisons onto the animal to soften its flesh, ready for eating!

I DON'T BELIEVE IT!

Female giant Pacific octopuses can lay up to 100,000 eggs at a time. They have 280 suckers on each tentacle, making 2240 in total. These monsters can swim to depths of 750 metres and can weigh as much as 180 kilograms!

44 **Southern stingrays feed primarily at night.** They have flat bodies that are almost invisible when lying on the seafloor. This helps them to hide from their main predators, such as hammerhead sharks. Stingrays have poor eyesight, but good senses of smell and touch, which they use to find crabs, shrimps and small fish when hunting at night.

45 **Cuttlefish use colourful displays to communicate with one another in dimly lit waters.** These molluscs are able to change the colour of their skin in seconds, producing a range of beautiful, shimmering and metallic shades. This also creates an effective camouflage – a handy way to avoid being eaten!

46 Most reptiles live in hot countries and many of them wait until the coolness of night to become active. Reptiles are animals with scaly skins that lay their eggs on land. There are four main groups of reptile – tortoises and turtles, lizards, snakes, and crocodiles and alligators.

◄ Tokay geckos are one of the largest geckos and they can be aggressive. They will attack other lizards and even bite humans who try to handle them. Tokay geckos can reach up to 35 centimetres in length and are usually brightly patterned.

47 Geckos are small nocturnal lizards that can climb walls and even walk upside down on ceilings. They have large eyes to help them see in the dark and thick toe pads that stick to surfaces. Tokay geckos from Southeast Asia are named after the loud 'to-kay' call males make, and they have unusually big yellow eyes.

48 Nocturnal snakes are superb hunters because their senses are so well adapted to detecting prey in the dark. Some snakes have an extra skill – they can feel the heat from another animal's body. Snakes, such as the western diamond rattlesnake, do this using special heat-detecting pits between their eyes and nostrils. Using this extra sense, the snake can find its prey in the dark and strike with deadly accuracy.

Heat-sensing pit

Body heat emitted from prey

The snake moves its head from side to side to locate its prey

▲ A western diamondback rattlesnake uses its heat-detecting pits to work out the distance and direction of its prey.

49 Some reptiles are huge and fearsome night-time hunters. Black caimans, which are members of the crocodile family, can reach 6 metres in length. They live in South America in freshwater rivers and lakes and at night they come to shallow water or land to hunt. Their dark skin colour means they can creep up on prey, such as deer or large rodents, unnoticed.

▼ During the day, common kraits are placid snakes and will rarely bite, even if disturbed. However at night they are more likely to be aggressive.

50 Common kraits are one of the deadliest snakes of Pakistan, India and Sri Lanka, and they are nocturnal. They prey on other snakes and rodents, sometimes straying into buildings to find them. Once they have found their prey, kraits lunge their fangs into it, injecting a lethal venom.

Whoo's there?

51 (Owls are nocturnal birds of prey with superb vision and excellent hearing.) Their eyes are large and face forwards, which helps them to judge distance. Their hearing is so good, they can locate their prey in total darkness just by listening!

52 The heart-shaped face of a barn owl works like a pair of ears! It helps to direct sound towards the sides of the owl's head, where the ears are situated at different heights. This helps them to pinpoint exactly where a sound is coming from. As they hover in the sky, barn owls can hear the tiny, high-pitched sounds made by small animals hidden in the vegetation below. Barn owls are able to fly almost silently towards their prey.

53 Barn owls are the most widespread land birds in the world and live on every continent, except Antarctica. They spend the day roosting (resting) in barns, buildings or trees and at night they come out to hunt. They catch rodents, such as rats, voles and mice.

I DON'T BELIEVE IT!

Barn owls have white undersides, which may not appear to be the best camouflage for a nocturnal animal. This actually helps them to disappear against the sky when seen from below, allowing them to stalk and attack their prey more easily.

▲ Barn owls have special adaptations that help them to hunt in the dark. Their soft feathers deaden the noise of flapping wings as they descend towards their unsuspecting prey.

54 Barn owls can see twice as well as humans by day and many times better at night. If an owl and a human were looking at the same image at night, the owl would see the image much more brightly. It would also be able to detect the smallest movement, which would be invisible to the human eye.

55 If they feel threatened or scared, owls slap their beaks together loudly making a clapping noise — this can sometimes be heard after dark. Barn owls shriek and hiss, but tawny owls are much more vocal. Their range of different calls can often be heard in the forests of Europe and Asia where they live. Male tawny owls make a loud 'hu-hooo' sound, which carries far in the still darkness. Females make a 'ke-wick' sound in reply. These noisy birds also make soft warbles and ear-piercing screeches!

Night fliers

56 **Owls are the best-known nocturnal birds, but there are others that also use the cover of darkness to hunt.** Many of them are so well adapted to life spent in the air that they can scarcely walk or hop. They sleep during the day, often roosting in trees, or hidden amongst plants on the ground.

▲ The gaping mouth of a nightjar acts like a net, catching insects as the bird flies.

▼ During the day, the common potoo mimics a branch to avoid the attention of predators.

57 **Nightjars are stocky birds with big mouths that fly at night with their beaks wide open to catch insects.** During the day, nightjars sleep on the ground or on low branches, without making nests. Their plumage – covering of feathers – is grey and brown, which camouflages them from predators, such as cats and foxes.

58 **Potoos are odd-looking nocturnal birds from Central and South America.** Their plumage is brown and they have yellow eyes. During the day they perch in trees, staying still with their eyes shut so that they may be mistaken for branches! At night, potoos dart through the sky gobbling up insects.

59 **Few birds sing at night, but the nightingale's song can be heard floating through the darkness.** The nightingale is known throughout the world for its beautiful song. Only male birds sing regularly after sunset and they use their songs of whistles, chirrups and trills to attract females.

◀ Frogmouths may attack and even kill other birds. They have very short legs and tiny feet.

▲ A nightingale's song is the only sign of this secretive bird's presence. Its dull colours keep it camouflaged.

HIDE ME, SEE ME!

Many animals are coloured or patterned in a way that helps them hide. This is called camouflage. But does it really work? Test it for yourself.

You will need:
thick, strong paper or card
paints or pens of different colours
scissors

Draw bold outlines of two birds. Colour one using bright, bold colours, but colour the other one in splodges of dull browns, greys and greens. Cut out your bird shapes and take them to a garden, park or woodland and hide them between plants. Which bird is easier to see?

60 **Frogmouths are nocturnal birds from Asia and Australia that hunt on the ground.** During the day they perch in trees, camouflaged by grey feathers mottled with dark stripes and blotches. A frogmouth's large, forward-facing eyes help it to spy prey at night, such as insects and small animals. Once prey is in sight, a frogmouth will pounce from its tree perch, capturing the animal in its beak.

Midnight marsupials

61 Kangaroos and koalas are marsupials, or pouched mammals, and most members of this group are nocturnal. There are about 196 types of marsupials living in and around Australia and about 85 types that live on the American continent. They are a strange group of animals that give birth to tiny youngsters that grow in a pouch on their mother's belly.

▼ Red kangaroos have a good sense of smell and they use it to find water in the Australian deserts.

62 Red kangaroos live in the great heat of the Australian outback where it's too hot for most animals to be active during the day. The red kangaroo is the world's largest marsupial. Its body reaches 1.6 metres in length and its tail is another 1.2 metres. It forages at night, nibbling at shoots, tender plants and leaves.

I DON'T BELIEVE IT!

Quolls are cat-like marsupials of Australia. They spend the night hunting, but during the day they like to sleep. Quolls find it difficult to nap if there's too much noise, so these clever creatures can fold their ears down to block out sound!

63 Koalas are bear-like marsupials that spend all day sleeping and all night eating. They eat and sleep up in the trees, and eucalyptus leaves are their main food. With stocky bodies, short limbs and leathery noses, koalas are easy to recognize.

64 **Virginia opossums forage at night and survive on all sorts of food, including grubs, fruit, eggs and scraps they scavenge from bins.** They live in North and Central America and shelter in piles of vegetation or under buildings. Opossums have an unusual skill – if they are scared they drop down and act dead, with their eyes and mouths open. They do this for up to six hours at a time – long enough for a predator to get bored and wander off!

▲ A Tasmanian devil gorges on its meal alone, but other devils may soon come to join in, drawn by the smell of fresh meat.

▼ A female Virginia opossum has up to 18 young in her litter, but she only has teats to feed 13 of them. She protects her young until they are old enough to fend for themselves.

65 **In Australia's southern island of Tasmania, a terrible screeching and barking may be heard in the night – a Tasmanian devil.** These marsupials are known for their noisy, aggressive behaviour and if they are alarmed, devils screech and bark. They can smell dead animals from far away and have such powerful jaws they can grind and chew bones and gristle.

66 Leaping between branches in moonlit forests requires excellent eyesight and fast reactions. These are qualities shared by many nocturnal primates. Lemurs, bushbabies, monkeys and apes are primates – intelligent mammals that have grasping hands and eyes that are set on the front of their faces.

▲ Owl, or night, monkeys are the only nocturnal monkeys of the Americas. They can see very well in the dark, thanks to their enormous eyes, but they are colour blind.

67 The only truly nocturnal monkeys are the night, or owl, monkeys, also called douroucoulis. Night monkeys have large owl-like eyes and small rounded heads. They feed on fruit, bugs, seeds and small animals. They howl, hoot and holler to communicate with one another in the darkness.

68 Mouse lemurs are the smallest of all primates and they are nocturnal. Some are only 18 centimetres long and weigh around 30 grams – about the same as four grapes! Mouse lemurs have very soft fur that is grey or orange-brown, with a black-and-white underneath. They live in trees and eat fruit, flowers, insects, spiders and occasionally frogs and lizards.

69 Bushbabies are small, furry animals that have huge eyes and can see well in the dark. They live in trees in the forests of East and central Africa. They run through the branches at night looking for insects, flowers, seeds and eggs to eat. During the day, bushbabies huddle together in hollow trees or sleep in old birds' nests.

70 As the sun sets on the island of Madagascar, the loud calls of ruffed lemurs can be heard across the treetops. These black-and-white, furry primates stay in touch with one another by making strange noises, which sound like someone laughing and screeching at the same time!

▶ Ruffed lemurs are most active at dawn and dusk, rather than through the night.

71 A slender loris uses all of its senses to guide it through the treetops at night. They are small primates that have huge eyes, nimble fingers and pointed noses. They live in India and Sri Lanka and they use stealth to hunt insects. A slender loris creeps up slowly and quietly behind its prey, sniffs its victim and then lunges, grabbing it in its hands.

◀ A slender loris measures no more than 26 centimetres in length and weighs around 300 grams. Its arms and legs are pencil-thin.

72 A flutter of wings and the glimpse of a swooping body in the night sky are often the only clues you'll get that a bat is nearby. Bats are the nocturnal masters of the sky. They are small, furry mammals that are so well adapted to life on the wing that they can pass by almost unnoticed by humans and animals alike.

▲ During the day, bats hang upside down and rest – this is called roosting.

73 Except for the polar regions, bats can be found all over the world. They roost in caves, trees, under logs and in buildings. There are nearly 1000 different types, or species, of bat – the smallest have wingspans of 15 centimetres, and the biggest have wingspans of 1.5 metres or more!

74 Bats are the only mammals that have wings. Their wings have developed from forelimbs and have a thin membrane of skin that stretches over long, bony digits, or fingers. Bats can change direction easily in flight, which helps them chase and catch insects.

I DON'T BELIEVE IT!

Bats can live for a surprisingly long time – often for 10 to 25 years. Some wild bats have been known to live to the ripe old age of 30! This is partly because bats are able to avoid being eaten as few animals can catch them when they dash and dart between trees.

75 Although bats have good eyesight, they depend more on their senses of smell and hearing to find their prey at night. Most types of bat have a special sense called echolocation. They produce very high-pitched sounds – too high for most people to hear – that bounce off objects in front of them. When the sound comes back to a bat's ears, like an echo, they can tell by the way it has changed, how far away the object is and its size.

76 There are two main groups of bat – plant-eating bats and hunting bats. Both groups are mainly nocturnal. However, it is the hunters that use echolocation to find their prey. Most plant eaters don't echolocate and tend to be bigger than hunting bats. Some plant-eating bats, such as the Rodrigues fruit bat, are active in the day. The word 'diurnal' (die-ur-nal) is used to describe creatures that are active during the day.

◄ The word 'sonic' means making sounds, and the high-pitched noises of bats can be described as 'ultrasonic' – too high for us to hear.

77 Oilbirds are unique – they are the world's only fruit-eating nocturnal birds, and they echolocate like bats. Oilbirds live in South America and they spend their days in total darkness, sleeping in pitch-black caves. They wake after sunset and travel up to 75 kilometres in search of food.

Echoes bouncing back off the moth

Sound waves from the bat

◄ Bats make high-pitched sounds, called clicks, using their mouths or noses. The sound hits an insect and bounces back to the bat's ears. The reflected sound gives the bat information about the location and size of the insect.

Insect eaters

78 Since many insects, grubs and worms are active night, so are the mammals that hunt them. Aardvarks are unusual ant-eating animals of Africa that snuffle and snort in the darkness. Their name means 'earth-pig' in Afrikaans, one of many languages spoken in South Africa, and they do look quite like long-nosed pigs with their big, fleshy snouts.

◄ Hedgehogs sleep during the day. At night, they come out to search for insects and worms to eat.

80 If they are scared, hedgehogs roll themselves into a tight ball with only their sharp spines showing. They may be able to defend themselves against foxes, but hedgehogs are no match for a car – thousands of these European mammals are killed on roads every year.

79 At night, aardvarks search for termites and ants using their good sense of smell as their eyesight is poor. They rip open nests and lick up the insects with their long tongues. Aardvarks also have large front claws, which they use for digging their burrows where they sleep during the day. They can close their ears and nostrils to stop dirt from getting in them as they dig.

◄ Aardvarks live alone and come out at sunset to forage for food. These long-snouted animals can eat up to 50,000 insects in one night!

81 Few people ever see pangolins as they are shy and secretive nocturnal creatures. Pangolins are armoured animals that live in Africa and Asia. Their bodies are covered in thick, overlapping scales, which are formed from layers of hardened skin. Pangolins don't have teeth, but lick up ants and termites with their long, sticky tongues.

▲ Pangolins have short legs and bodies measuring up to one metre in length. They can climb trees or dig burrows underground using their long, sharp claws.

82 Shrews are active by night as well as day, since they must eat every few hours to survive. They are mouse-like, furry creatures with long snouts and are some of the smallest mammals in the world. They rely mostly on their sense of smell to find food, but some of them use echolocation – a way of locating objects using sound that is used by bats and oilbirds.

◄ A tiny shrew prepares to devour an earthworm, which looks like a giant in comparison.

Chisellers and chewers

83 **Some of the world's commonest mammals are nocturnal rodents such as mice, rats, voles and lemmings.** This group of animals can exist in almost any habitat all over the world, except the Antarctic. They have big eyes to see in the dark, furry bodies, and teeth that are perfect for gnawing and chewing. Most also have good hearing, and long whiskers to feel their way in the dark.

▼ At night, rats roam around towns scavenging any food and scraps they can find.

84 **Rats are active in the day, but more so at night.** They are experts in survival – able to live almost anywhere. One of the reasons for their success is that they can eat nearly anything. Rats hunt for food but they are just as likely to scavenge rubbish from bins at night or find morsels in the sewers. These unpopular animals have been known to start eating the flesh of living things and spread deadly diseases.

85 Giant flying squirrels emerge from their tree holes at night and search for nuts, berries and shoots. They can 'fly' between trees by stretching out thin membranes of skin between their limbs, allowing them to glide through the air.

86 American beavers are large rodents, often measuring more than one metre in length from nose to tail-tip. They spend the day resting in a lodge, which is a nest made from mud and sticks with underwater entrances. Beavers leave their nests as the sun begins to set and they remain busy through much of the night, feeding on plants. They find their way around using their long whiskers to guide them.

▼ Beavers chisel at trees and branches, cutting them up for use in the dams they build on rivers and streams. These dams create wetlands where many types of animal and plant thrive.

87 Edible dormice are small, nocturnal rodents that live in woods, or make their nests near or under buildings. During the late summer and autumn they fatten themselves up with seeds, fruit and nuts to prepare for hibernation – a long winter sleep. The ancient Romans kept edible dormice and overfed them until they were so fat they could hardly move. They were cooked until crisp and crunchy and served at dinners and parties!

Death by stealth

▶ The serval is a member of the cat family that lives in Africa. Its large eyes help it to see prey in the dim light of the setting sun.

88 Hunting at night provides a perfect opportunity for carnivores to pounce on their prey, unseen and undetected. The word 'carnivore' describes meat-eating animals, and members of the cat family are amongst the most agile and elegant of them all.

▼ The glow from the eyes of these lions comes from the tapetum – a layer of light-reflecting cells that all cats have in their eyeballs.

89 Wildcats are the ancestors of domestic, or pet, cats. Like domestic cats, wildcats are active at night as well as during the day, but they do most of their hunting at night. They look like large, stocky tabby cats with black-tipped, bushy tails. They eat small rodents, rabbits and birds.

90 Many big cats choose the twilight hours – dawn and dusk – to look for food. Most live in places where the day's heat is too great for stalking and running. Cool nights are more comfortable for most animals, including prey animals such as antelope and deer that gather at waterholes or riversides. Big cats will sometimes lie in wait there – their tawny, stripy or spotty coats helping them to stay hidden in the shadows.

91 Leopards can hunt in the day or at night, but are more likely to be successful when the light is low. These strong, solitary animals are the most widespread of all big cats. Part of their success is due to their supreme hunting skills and the wide range of food they will eat. One clever leopard tactic is to ambush a group of baboons as they sleep at night – too startled to fight or run, the monkeys make sitting targets.

QUIZ

1. What name is given to animals that are active in the day – diurnal or eternal?
2. What is a carnivore – a meat eater or a plant eater?
3. What name is given to an animal that preys upon, or hunts, others – prefect or predator?

Answers:
1. Diurnal 2. A meat eater 3. Predator

92 Wolves are carnivores and, like many other members of the dog family, they are nocturnal. Using their strong sense of smell wolves are able to detect animals, such as deer, moose, rabbits or beavers, and follow their scent trail for many kilometres. Wolves will always choose the weakest member of a herd to attack and they know to approach their prey from downwind so that it does not smell them!

▼ Wolves live in the far north, where night-time can last 20 hours or more during the long, cold winters.

The African plains

93 At dusk on the African grassland, diurnal (daytime) animals visit waterholes before resting for the night, and nocturnal animals become active. Hippopotamuses aren't everyone's idea of nocturnal creatures, but these huge mammals have very sensitive skin that easily burns in the hot sun. They spend the day wallowing in cool pools and come onto land at night to feed.

94 Hippos are plant eaters and spend the night chewing on plants at the waterside. They grunt and snuffle like pigs as they graze, eating up to 40 kilograms of plants and grass every night. Like lots of other nocturnal animals, hippos don't sleep all day, but have active times mixed with long naps.

▲ As the sun disappears behind the horizon, hippos amble onto the shore to graze on grass for most of the night.

95 Rhinos are another animal of the African plains that prefer to feed once the sun has set and it is cool. These enormous plant eaters have poor eyesight and depend on their excellent sense of smell to find food and sense predators. By day they rest in the shade or bathe in mud to keep cool.

▲ At night, rhinoceroses rely on their senses of smell and hearing to stay safe from predators. They mainly eat grass, but will also eat fruit, leaves and crops.

96 Spotted hyenas are night-time hunters of the African grasslands. They are most active after dusk, and spend the day in burrows that they have either dug themselves, or have taken over from aardvarks or warthogs. Hyenas call to one another at night with a whooping noise. These calls show obedience to a senior member of the group.

▶ Hyenas can ambush and kill large animals because they work together in groups. They have excellent senses of sight, hearing and smell.

A new day dawns

97 As night draws to an end, nocturnal creatures head back to their dens and burrows. Smaller animals steal away to hide beneath rocks, in caves or under plants. With their stomachs full it's time to rest and stay safe – and that means remaining hidden from view.

▶ Flying foxes, or fruit bats, are nocturnal plant-eating bats. During the day, they roost, hanging upside down by their feet from tree branches, in groups that sometimes number several thousand.

98 The break of dawn is a time of great activity and noise. Nocturnal animals are gradually replaced by diurnal ones. Birds announce the sunrise with their songs and bats can still be seen flitting around amongst the treetops, snatching insects out of the air. Lions laze around, having spent the night roaming the plains hunting, eating and napping. Cubs play in the cool air and perhaps wander to a waterhole to take a drink, before the whole pride settles down to a morning snooze.

WORD GAME

How many words can you make from the letters in the word NOCTURNAL? You should be able to find the names of three animals that you have read about in this book!

99 Domestic cats are expert hunters and are most active in the twilight hours. Their well-developed senses of sight, hearing, taste and touch make them successful night-time hunters. They often return to their homes with small rodents, birds or insects they have caught in the night. Domestic cats usually spend the day sleeping and lazing around.

100 In rainforests and woodlands, morning dew drips from leaves as owls cease their hooting and foxes fall silent. Rodents scurry out of the light, seeking safety under stones or in cracks in tree trunks, and owls return to their treeholes. Now, diurnal birds of prey, such as eagles and hawks, hover in the sky, on the lookout for small rodents far below.

▼ European badgers snuggle together in their dens, called setts, to keep warm. They spend most of the day asleep.

▲ These young tawny owls have a safe place to hide during daylight hours. In this treehole, they are out of the reach of predators and protected from bad weather.

Index

Entries in **bold** refer to main subject entries.
Entries in *italics* refer to illustrations.